Your H

Your Highest Potential

The New Psychology
of Understanding and Working with Self

Annette Colby, PhD

Your Highest Potential

© 2007 Annette Colby

Manufactured in the United States of America

For information, please contact:
Brown Books Publishing Group
16200 North Dallas Parkway, Suite 170
Dallas, Texas 75248
www.brownbooks.com
972-381-0009
A New Era in Publishing™

ISBN-13: 978-1-933285-93-1
ISBN-10: 1-933285-93-1
LCCN 2007904061
1 2 3 4 5 6 7 8 9 10

Dedicated to the
evolution of a
joyful human experience

Contents

Acknowledgments

To my husband Ray Nowicki, for his contagiously generous laughter and love, for sharing his enthusiastic zest for life with me, and with whom I want to build great new potentials for the rest of my life!

To Adrienne Cocita, whose life-long friendship fills my every day with sunshine.

To Terry Colby, who offered unconditional and unwavering benevolence and always saw the "diamond within."

chapter one

Remembering Self

Once, a long time ago, a girl stood at the edge of a garden, lost and confused. Warm tears of defeat stained the earth as the child felt herself giving up. She looked toward the heavens and asked to return. Her heart, heavy with pain and sadness, had decided that coming to Earth had been a mistake. The little girl prayed, "Dear Heaven, please, please hear me. My heart is very sad. I don't know how to bring my message of love to this place. Will you please take me back?"

Waiting, she heard nothing above the crushing emptiness of her despair. The sky did not open. Angels with feathery wings did not descend to scoop her up. From the depths of loneliness, the child cried, "Will no one comfort me, speak to me, or take away my pain? What sin have I committed that I would be cast out and left here alone?"

She stood silently in the garden and heard no voice of instruction, no singing angels. In the silence, her heart was broken by this abandonment. She made a decision straight from the imagination of a child. She decided that the love she embodied meant nothing, had no value, and held no power here on Earth. She decided that being left here on Earth was punishment, and her heart shattered.

The child in the story was five years old. I was that lost spirit. It was a dilemma. The world's prevailing ideas, traditions, and beliefs made no sense to me. I felt I had no power to effect change—and yet leaving was not an available option. I was confused. I felt alone and different and eccentric.

The psychological thriller *The Sixth Sense*, written and directed by M. Night Shyamalan, tells the tale of an eccentric eight-year-old boy, Cole, who is haunted by his inborn gift: he is visited by ghosts. Cole is terrified of his gift and eventually confides, "I see dead people." Confused by his paranormal powers, Cole is too young to understand his purpose and too afraid to tell anyone about his terror. Through the movie, the boy goes on a journey to overcome his fears, all the while discovering the purpose of his gift.

Like this movie, I was born with a gift that frightened me as much as Cole's ability to see ghosts frightened him. No, I do

  2

not see ghosts. And no, my journey of overcoming my fear and understanding my purpose was not resolved in the span of a two-hour movie. As I child, I was confused. I was too young to understand what I sensed and too immature to put it into words. I was terrified to share my secret with anyone.

What is my gift? Ironically, I could also say I "see dead people" but not because I see ghosts. Instead, I see people walking around in human bodies, carrying their inner pain, suffering helplessly, disconnected from the spirit realm. I see people who have abandoned their purpose, living in this physical reality but forgetting to combine their life with love of self. I see that there are two worlds: the physical world and the spirit realm and that without a bridge between our physical self and our spirit self, life is filled with meaningless anguish and suffering.

I do not just see this. I feel it. When I am around someone, I sense their inner anguish inside my own flesh and bones and spirit. I sense how they put on a show of expression and yet carry their stress and suffering inside. I sense their heaviness, their lack of life energy, and their inability to connect their human suffering with their spirit. I am acutely aware of how people shield themselves, block access to their hearts, and try to hide their fear.

I believed that people should be feeling gladder to be alive. They should have more joy in their bodies for themselves and to share with the people around them. There is a beauty to life that people are missing. There is mystery, wonder, and magnificence available. Everything is a process of creativity and expansion. I believed people could be living each day liberating from oppression, putting effort into feeling better, nurturing greatness in themselves, and lifting up the people they claimed to love. They could be moving decidedly toward greater peace and harmony. Tomorrow could be better than today.

Back in my formative years, I was too young to understand what I felt and sensed. The people I loved were hurting and I could not help them. I was unable to express my understandings in any useful fashion. I suppose I also thought my vision should already exist here on Earth. I did not know that my purpose was to use my gift of empathy to help people form a richer fuller connection between life and spirit. Lacking the maturity to handle my gift and knowing no other way to deal with my confusion and sense of failure, at five years old, I simply surrendered.

Life went on for me, but with one huge difference. My visions, my concepts, my feelings, and my light were tucked away within my body in places no one was allowed to enter. Facing an external world that was the antithesis of my internal vision, my response was to live an intellectual existence. I did the best I could within the rigid rules, authoritarian structure, and assigned roles of the surrounding system. No longer focused on my inner truths or desires, my mind was now preoccupied with learning to meet other people's expectations. I made countless decisions about my power, my visions, my voice, my passionate spontaneity, and my love that would guide my life for many years to come.

My self-created dogma told me I was unacceptable in any realm: Heaven or Earth. I began to convince myself that perhaps somewhere, in some other time or place, I had committed a crime so horrible no one would even remind me of what it was. Or perhaps something was wrong with my appearance, my face or my physical body, that made my inner world invisible to others. An abandoned heart was my punishment for this litany of fabricated sins. Each successive painful emotional experience confirmed these ideas and made them seem more real. As long as my mind could fuel a constant stream of things that were wrong with me, then it could attempt to keep the "unacceptable" aspects of myself hidden away.

I thought my prayer would be answered instantly in a glorious blaze of light and feathers. When this did not happen, many of the beliefs I was already forming about myself became concrete. I now had further proof that I was powerless on Earth.

My feelings that people could move beyond their personal dramas and use their inner abilities to create joyful lives, loving partnerships, and expand their abundance were meaningless. I still held my visions of an amazing Earth where individuals accepted their empowerment, fuelled their creative expressions with love and passion, and they were glad to be alive in human bodies while contributing to the joy of others around them. Yet I had already convinced myself that my visions did not stand a chance of being expressed. These visions were carefully locked away while I added new beliefs that the possibilities I saw for life were inconsequential.

I stayed quiet, well-behaved, and almost nonexistent. I was able to succeed in the world by memorizing and adhering to the world's rules. The system worked well enough in terms of fitting in and meeting other people's expectations. Yet, changing my outer self to fit the existing system did not work inside. It was impossible to ignore what I knew and what I felt. Pushing down what I knew to be truth, dissociating from my own love of self, and failing to express my authenticity left life devoid of meaning. I now carried a deep sadness, feeling like an insignificant outsider with no ability to bring my inner ideas into the world.

Needless to say, my initial way of coping did not work well over time, but what else was there? Perplexed by the world and

attempting to suppress my own identity, I was nonetheless filled with life and creative energy. All of this energy swirled and wanted an outlet, but it had no avenue of self-directed, authentic expression. For any of us, energy without direction does not feel good, and our bodies send intense signals of emotional pain. In adolescence, my self-created system began to break down. Unable to handle the emotions (for that is the heart's job), my mind kicked into overdrive, inventing new ways to "fix" the pain and push it away. Intellectual achievement, staying busy, challenging my body image, perfectionism, and obsessive behavior became important new coping strategies to drown out the pain of self-oppression. When those methods failed to stop the rising energy of self, various addictions began to creep in. All were strategies unconsciously chosen to suppress self-expression, numb the conflict I had created, and ignore my body's messages.

The specific details of my young sorrow might be unique, but the experiences of pain, being different, disappointment, and powerlessness have not been strangers to any of us. Life's journey into the infinite layers of our own heart is deep and endless. In all times, throughout the ages, each individual must face his or her individual quest for the meaning of life. It is the hardships we face, the emotional traumas, or the events beyond comprehension that lead us to deep, personal questions such as, Who am I?, Why am I on Earth?, What is my purpose?, What is my relationship to God?, and What power do I have to effect change?

Life's joys and sorrows bring us unique opportunities to expand our comprehension of ourselves as creative beings of light and love. Challenging situations allow us to reach deep inside and take responsibility to bring change to our lives. As we accept the journey of creating change, we achieve a higher potential on all levels of being—physical, mental, emotional, and spiritual. It is our decision to lead ourselves through difficult times that offers the promise of evolution.

Sometimes when a difficult challenge occurs, we are able to sustain belief in ourselves. No matter what is going on in the outer world, we do not lose sight of our importance and value, our dreams, our love, and our capacity to ultimately achieve a successful outcome. Somehow, we persevere. Despite crisis, we avoid falling into helpless despair. We make conscious choices not to abandon ourselves and to stay true to our inner truths and desires.

If we remain solid in our belief in self and in love, we discover intuitive resolutions and unveil hidden talents and strengths. In the process, we create more intimate relationships with ourselves and with those around us. Love expands, inner peace deepens, and harmony with self and all of creation increases. Personal evolution accelerates as we learn to trust our ability to imagine creative outcomes and physically manifest our desires. Inner joy expands as we realize we possess the capacity to imagine, create, receive, and live an exciting life. The successful navigation of a life challenge increases our trust of life, our love of self, and leads us closer to understanding our purpose for being alive.

Other times, our challenges bring us to our knees. The darkness of some situations overwhelms us; life's turbulence leaves us off-balance. Life seems chaotic and without purpose. Not knowing how to navigate the crisis, we inadvertently allow fear, doubt, and anxiety to consume us. Matters worsen as we are now cut off from connection with love and creative solutions. Feeling a lack of personal empowerment, we believe we are unable to exert control over our personal direction in life. We mistakenly conclude we can't affect the future. Because of this chain of events, we feel unsupported, inadequate, and alone. We may even feel abandoned by God. Seeing no other course of action we may decide to withdraw from life. In essence, we become trapped in our illusions of powerlessness.

In truth, at any given moment we have access to creative thought, inner passion, and the ability to lead ourselves successfully through any difficulty into a more desirable real-

ity. Unfortunately, especially in times of crisis, difficulty, or change, we do not know how to lift out of the world of struggle and tap into the energy of higher potential. Instead of rising above the conflict, developing imaginative solutions, and empowering ourselves with creative passion, we end up perpetually stuck fighting our realities or succumbing to them.

Decisions

We come into the world warm and open with soft, flexible, little bodies, exposed and vulnerable, expecting to be touched and nurtured in all the ways that feel good. Our eyes are wide open, eagerly looking into this magical place, and ready to explore. As we gain self-awareness, we attempt to make sense of our environment and make decisions about how we fit within it.

During the early stages of life, we survive by integrating with our family and with society. Young children conform to familial and cultural values, and they surrender access to some of their own inner wisdom. Discipline and orderliness take their places above being a free spirit. Through many experiences, children make decisions about how freely and passionately they express themselves, their love, and their creativity. Some of us become aloof while others become intimidating; some develop victim strategies while others develop righteousness. Decisions are made about the importance of conformity, social approval, and adapting to society's thoughts and ideals. We decide whether we are wanted and desirable, supported and secure. Ideas are formed about whether we are part of the collective Earth, and if we have the right to be ourselves.

Each of us, to some extent, puts aside personal desires as we adopt strategies to deal with a pre-existing world. Carefully, we watch how the family, religious, and society systems of our world operate. Using intelligence we observe, analyze, and decide what to believe about ourselves in certain situations. We choose how we will respond. Slowly, throughout our formative years, we trade authentic expression and create what we believe to be an acceptable personality that blends in. This suitable personality has a certain way of thinking, acting, and behaving.

While many of these developmental beliefs help us survive in the existing world, they do so with the ideas that certain aspects of our selves are unimportant, shameful, or unacceptable. Though these beliefs may have helped us early on within our own family's dynamic, now these beliefs form barriers that block joy, love, and authentic self-expression. Such bar-

riers can lead to pessimism, inaction, and depression.

We are always creating our reality, even though we may be consciously unaware of how we are contributing to the formation of the world around us. For example, while we are growing up, we encounter difficult life challenges. In our infinite ability to create, we concoct elaborate explanations for things we do not understand, or why we feel powerless, alone, or frightened. We decide we are the cause of the situation, and if we were somehow different, then the situation would go away. Based on these beliefs, we develop complex strategies that enable us to adapt. Whether or not the situation goes away, we do survive because of the beliefs we created. Over time, these beliefs and action strategies become hardwired into our minds and bodies.

As a five-year-old, I had already made decisions about my worth. The experiences I had, or did not have, confirmed what I was thinking, and these thoughts became beliefs and life's constant companions. Emotional pain welds beliefs deep into the psyche until they are physically embedded. It is the same for all of us. Over time, our beliefs become the bedrock upon which we construct our entire lives. They work overtime to keep us safe, dictating behaviors that gain approval, acceptance, power, and love from the people in our lives.

This is an amazingly creative undertaking! However, once we have formed certain beliefs, certain ways of acting, and a certain personality, we tend to remain operating from within that self-assigned structure. Gradually, we trade our ability to be spontaneous, authentic, and creative, for the safety of living within our belief structure. We go through life and bring our highly formed beliefs and personalities with us into every new situation. Not surprisingly, these ways of being generate predictable outcomes. They may or may not be the best possible outcomes, but they are most certainly outcomes in which we survive.

For many people, hiding authentic expression and inborn ideas of how the world could be seemed to be the best available option at the time to survive and protect themselves. It was a way of surviving in a world that appeared, at first glance, to be limited and based on performance, conformity, or obedience. While safeguarding authentic self-expression might have been seen as the best choice available to us as children, the side effect is that we wander about, feeling empty, dispassionate, or disconnected. Something seems to be missing, like some information or piece of ourselves that would make us solid and complete once more.

The belief systems we create in youth serve us by keeping our authenticity hidden and protected. As a result, we lose faith in

many vital aspects of the self: our bodies, our inner wisdom, our passion, our emotions and feelings, our intuition, and our inner knowing. We forget how we would live in the world and how we would create the world around us if we were left to our own imagination and love. This self-created system of self-control allows us to set purely logical goals and to create a seemingly "good" life. Strategies formed during youth may lead to a life that appears successful on the surface, but feels less than fully alive on the inside.

On the inside, we may be feeling the pain of inertia. Our personal evolution is no longer moving forward as we remain within the box created by our beliefs. This box has become too small and limiting. We get a sense that we could be more; we could create something new once again. Yet, since we have effectively survived, we feel we have no other choice than to continue living by our patterns. We give our minds the job of remaining "in control" by continuously enforcing our beliefs. The downside is that we fail to take risks, set goals, or trust ourselves to imagine new outcomes. Our hearts are no longer wide open to spontaneity and creativity, and our bodies become frozen to authentic expression of self. Life becomes a pattern of performing and achieving, following the rules, and trying hard to please.

However, inner desire is always present; desire to imagine

exciting outcomes, desire to change inertia, and the desire for passionate authentic expression. We sense the stirring of desire within and feel the discomfort of the life we are living. We feel the longing to create a new potential for ourselves. Yet, it is often not until years later that we find the courage to stop suppressing the desire to create change. By setting goals, we begin the process of shedding conformist ideas and tapping back into individual passions and dreams. Our journey of personal evolution has begun once again.

In the beginning, the logical mind is eager to go on this personal growth journey—only because it thinks it can perfect the "acceptable personality" that has been previously formed. The mind loves the work of growth and spiritual expansion. It keeps us busy attempting to "fix" ourselves. It is a trick, of sorts, as the logical mind attempts only to strengthen conformity so we can fit in even better. The mind tries to manufacture a person who never fails, who never feels sad or bad, a person loved, admired, and respected by other people, a person who can keep others happy.

Over time we begin to see through the intellectual pursuit. The real intention of any personal growth or spiritual journey is not to figure out what is wrong with us, to fix ourselves, or to fit more perfectly into the prevailing way of life. Instead, personal evolution is about moving forward, trusting our feel-

ings and emotions, taking risks, and doing things we have never done before. It's about moving beyond what we have learned.

We all learn the dance of life from someone else. We study the steps and conform to the dance that is taught to us. There is nothing wrong or broken about us for having learned a certain way of dancing through life. Yet, now it is time to feel the music of life and create our own dance. The emotional pain we feel is the realization that we have more to contribute to life than our current beliefs allow. That pain is wonderful for it propels us to take responsibility for our lives and create new outcomes. We no longer have to follow the path of conformity. Yes, it is scary to open our hearts once more, but we are born to bring new ideas to life and live excitedly within our bodies. Our highest potential is the decision to take one more step into our own ability to join spirit and flesh, and create a new experience for ourselves.

Imagination

The road to discovering a meaningful and fulfilling life requires facing the reality of the situations we encountered while growing up. It also requires facing that we alone created our own decisions, created our own beliefs systems, and developed certain behavior habits based on interplay between life experiences and our own inborn temperaments and personality traits.

Temperaments are how we interact with the world and how we approach things. We may be cautious or direct, calm or anxious, curious or slow-to-warm-up, easygoing or fearful, independent or willing-to-please. Temperaments combined with experiences dictated which aspects of ourselves we pushed aside or deemed unworthy, and which aspects of self we allowed into existence.

Our past life experiences remain unalterable. The point is not to blame our parents or ourselves, but to accept reality. The greater life, the happier life, the more abundant life we want to live is still available to us. Old decisions cannot be changed and no one can undo the past, but we can make new decisions, develop self-supporting habits, and form new belief systems. It is possible for anyone who desires to move up in the continuum of happiness and fulfilment.

Certain individuals are more aware of the internal conflict between who they have become and who they want to be. They feel lonely, empty, and aware that something is missing from their lives. They feel a powerful stirring inside, an inner call

to be more alive than what they are. They seek something they cannot define, and it is a loving connection between self and new self-expression. Their beliefs created a need to abandon certain aspects of themselves, such as the parts that contained life energy, intuition, creativity, originality, and joy. Even though we might have put certain aspects of ourselves into hiding, they are still alive. Now these aspects of self are ready to be uncovered, empowered, and allowed avenues of creative expression. The pain of this conflict is an important call to bring balance back into life.

How do we trust these suppressed parts of ourselves once again? The answer lies in a powerful combination of deciphering the language of our emotions and then engaging the imagination. In the big picture, emotional pain is a beautiful and important red flag. It is an alarm signalling the arrival of personal evolution. Painful emotions tell us that we cannot live like this anymore. It is time to move beyond survival. Emotions show us very clearly that our beliefs and habitual actions no longer work. It is time to love ourselves and open the narrow box where life-energy, imagination, intuition, passion, creativity, and authentic self-expression have been stored! Emotions tell us, "I don't want this experience anymore." Emotions tell us what is real right now and inform us of what we have outgrown. Imagination however tells us, "I would rather choose to have this particular experience."

Unfortunately, many people have taught themselves to deactivate their imaginations, not realizing that it is the crucial ingredient required to create a happier life. Imagination is the bridge we construct between the physical and the spiritual. On this bridge, we connect with preferred outcomes, engage in a process of expanding those desires, and then to allow those desires to travel back across into the physical world. Imagination lifts us out of the problem and connects us with our spirit's exciting make-believe hopes and ethereal dreams not yet in existence. Imagination allows the formation of a loving relationship with what is wanted, but is not yet true.

Imagination allows the continuous expansion of our spirit by extending past the cocoon of survival strategies and self-imposed limitations. Regardless of what faith, theologies, or spiritual beliefs we hold, we all have an authentic God-self within and an individual purpose for being here. This purpose is realized as we align with ideas that spark the imagination and align with ideas that bring greater joy into physical form.

Like snowflakes, each individual holds a pattern of unique dreams and desires. As children, we might have decided that our own unique pattern is too different from those around us. In an attempt to blend in, we invented a costume, different from ourselves, patterned after the personality traits we thought others desired to see in us. Still, beneath the costume lies the unchangeable essence of who we are. Emotions tell us it is time to shed the costume, while imagination tells us what life would be like if we could design it ourselves.

Self-Expression

Our singular journey is neither to judge the paths that others take, nor perpetually follow the path laid out by others. Instead, our life journey is to seek purpose, alignment with personal values and preferences, and creative self-expression. We need to forget trying to rescue the world, for we have a far more important mission. Our mission is to trust ourselves to listen to the wisdom of our emotions, utilize imagination to design meaningful outcomes, put joy into the creation of those outcomes, and then live the expression of our desires. Our natural drive for the fullest possible self-expression leads to renewed vitality, choosing challenges that stimulate growth, and committing ourselves to betterment of humanity.

By deciding to live a life of personally meaningful self-expression, we activate our own personal life energy and develop a heart-felt connection with life. Suddenly we begin

to enjoy living in a body! We anticipate the arrival of a new day! In addition, quite surprisingly, we begin to notice that we influence the lives of others. As we become more excited about being alive, with a finer spirit of hope and achievement, more passionate in our actions, and more empowered, we spread a new potential into the world. When we dare to live with greater vision and develop a burning passion to express ourselves creatively, we inspire others to wake up their own unique self-expression.

A great difference is obvious when we compare the amount of inspiration a shy wallflower gives to the world in contrast to that given by an inspired musician. The person standing quietly against the wall is withdrawn, pulled in, and barely visible. In contrast, the melody coming from the musician is physically and energetically alive, penetrating everyone in the room with its heartbeat. It is not wrong to be a shy wallflower at times, but what does not feel good is permanently hiding our inner visions and never being able to share them with the world because we fear that our expression would be judged and rejected, or that it might make someone else unhappy. When I am fearful that my inner truths are of no consequence and not worth expressing, I am reminded by Gandhi's words, "Whatever you do may seem insignificant, but it is most important that you do it."

Self-expression is the ability to find our inner heart messages and release them into the world without reservation. Soul-centered leadership depends on our freedom to consciously express the uniqueness and sacredness of our individuality. It does not matter if someone "likes" or "dislikes" our expression for that is not why we express ourselves. What matters is our ability to reach into our inner realms and ask, "What do I believe in my heart?" Only then are we able to express ourselves in a manner that will enrich the world and enhance our joy.

Joy is the ability to look within, see a vision, an idea, or a desire, and then find an imaginative way to articulate this on the outside. "I can see it inside. How do I find a form of expression to accurately convey my meaning?" Joy is the harmony of the inner vision with the outer expression. Joy is not the approval given to us by another. It is not the outer validation that our writing, art, visions, or expression is "good." Joy is when we know, when we can feel the resonance with every fiber in our body, that equality has been established between our inner concept and an outer physical reflection. American painter Edward Hopper responded once, "If I could say it in words there would be no reason to paint." Self-expression requires imagination and passion so that we may find our most suitable form of expression through verbal communication, writing, art, music, science, mathematics, or abstract expression.

Henry Van Dyke, the late American author and clergyman, shared much wisdom when he stated, "Use what talents you possess: the woods would be very silent if no birds sang there except those that sang best." We have within us the ability to shine, to love, and to create a personally meaningful life. We have the capacity to receive love so fully that it overflows from within us like light from the sun overflows onto Earth. The sun does not share its light for any purpose; it is neither trying to get approval and acceptance, nor worrying about being too hot, too dangerous, or too bright. The sun does not say to itself, "Oh no, I am causing skin cancer in some people. I am causing other people to sweat and complain. I am going to have to tone down. I am ashamed of myself." The sun bears no responsibility to us; it simply shines, living its purpose, and is unconcerned that its light creates and sustains life. In a similar manner, our primary function is to light ourselves up from the inside, shining because we are meant to shine. In the process, a few others might complain and disapprove, but most will see a living model of what is possible for humanity and become inspired.

No one outside of us has the ability to open the door to our self-expression, and no outsider has the ability to close it. If we courageously confront the fear of being ourselves and expand self-confidence to express our heart-felt inner truths,

we realize an amazing discovery: the differences that we once sought to cover up are the expressions that make our life worth living and change the lives of others. As we free ourselves from limiting beliefs and decide that our inner ideas are worth expressing, we begin to shine. Other people notice our passion for life and wonder if they also could become more radiant!

Gaining Personal Power

You are not powerless to affect change and neither am I. But sometimes it certainly feels that way. In the classic tale, "The Ugly Duckling" by Hans Christian Andersen, the poor baby swan-to-be had no idea that he really could be a part of the world, that he could fly, or that he was really a swan and not a duck. For a period of his life, he was convinced he was destined to be nothing more than a rejected and lonely outcast. How wrong he was! Through his journey, he discovers his true identity and realizes that he had never been an ugly duckling after all. Just like in the journey of the baby swan, your personal power is waiting for discovery.

Personal power has many definitions, but in essence, personal power is the ability to achieve what is wanted from conception to completion. When we know we can do anything we set our minds to do, and we do so with inner peace and excitement as our companions, then we have personal power.

In contrast, a sense of powerlessness occurs when we believe we have no authority over our own emotions, happiness, or desires. We mistakenly believe we cannot create exciting outcomes in our own lives. Therefore, we accept our fate and take what life dishes out. Acquiescing to our unhappy situation it is easy to blame others for our sense of being unfulfilled. We may act out, rage, weep, mourn, or drown our sorrows in addiction. Yet, without an adequate supply of personal power, we can easily become caught in the drama of complaining about our circumstances, without having the ability to lift out of them.

Everyone has personal power. It is flowing through your veins right now. The real issue is learning to access the amount of personal power currently available and then increase our supply. The first action involves deciding that you want empowerment, allowing it, and finding yourself worthy of having it. Then, to increase how much internal power is available, you decide to set specific and meaningful goals and then accomplish them. This journey of setting and achieving goals is how you discover that you do indeed have the inner power to effect change in your own life, family, community, and world.

Instead of giving power away to undesired emotions and circumstances, power involves conscious will to form your own destiny, bring your dreams up to the forefront, and happily dwell on anticipated success. You gain personal power when you look at your present life-circumstances and take responsibility to decide exactly what is wanted. Then, even though you do not know if you will fail or succeed, you move forward. You learn to say "yes" to actions that support your decision, and "no" to actions that sabotage. Amazingly, just like the ugly duckling, you discover that personal power is not dependent on anyone or anything outside of one's self. You had it all along!

By imagining desired outcomes, you give yourself permission to get involved in your own life and to take responsibility for feeling good in your body. Rather than constant worry about what is currently happening, the focus shifts to imaginary desired solutions. Remember, everything in life begins first with an imagined vision and a connection between the physical you and the spirit you. Instead of apathy with the way things are, or blaming others, we take initiative for our own happiness by deciding to concentrate on pleasing outcomes.

Sometimes we give away our personal power. One such example is when we use our available inner power for protection

 26

or conformity. Power that is used for survival is not available for growth and expansion. Freeing this inner power means intentionally choosing to go beyond surviving and coping to thriving by deciding to create change. Making the choice to create something that did not formerly exist will ultimately lead you directly into your own sense of powerlessness. As uncomfortable and difficult to confront as it may sound, that is the journey that must be taken. New energy, new ideas, new beliefs, and new choices must be introduced onto this arid landscape of perceived powerlessness before you can discover that the power to create was yours all along.

Your inner sense of powerlessness is like a desert: barren, scorched, and desolate. It is a wasteland lacking both the seeds of alternate possibilities, and the water necessary to grow new potentials. It is impossible for new potentials to grow here on their own accord. Determined effort is required. Vultures of limiting beliefs also live in this desert of perceived power-lessness. These dark beliefs circle about, waiting to devour any seedling that happens to sprout. They circle overhead, screeching that we cannot have what we want, hissing our inadequacy. Tremendous courage is required to enter this land of perceived powerlessness, fear, and painful beliefs while resisting the urge to run, hide, or surrender to the old beliefs in apathy, despair, or depression.

This forlorn, solitary desert of perceived powerlessness must be faced before the promise of a new life begins. It is into this desert that new beliefs must be introduced. Power *begins* as we dare to bring our dreams and ourselves into this desert landscape of perceived powerlessness. Power *develops* as we draw on inner strengths when things are not going well. Power *expands* as we discover we are capable of encountering difficulties without collapsing or raging. We stand strong in the desert, plant our dreams, and despite the doubts and fears of our limiting beliefs, we allow creative thought, intuition, and love for self back into our body and, subsequently, the world.

It may take a while for these newly released dreams to take root so do not abandon them too quickly. Remain steadfast while pumping the water of passion onto your newly planted dreams. Personal power is yours as you dare the actions of tending to your dreams, even while the surrounding reality of your life is currently a barren desert.

Personal power is not power over anyone, nor is it gained by standing against anything, anyone, or any situation. It is not gained by anger or blame at anyone, even blaming ourselves, for the current circumstances of life. We have power beyond our wildest dreams, and we can do things we never thought possible. However, we must discover this for ourselves, and we do so by choosing to face challenges in new ways.

Power develops by learning to value what does not feel good as an important source of information about what is not wanted, and then utilizing this information to form ideas about what would feel good and what is wanted. We can lift our consciousness and focus on desired outcomes instead of dwelling in current stress or sorrow. We have operated on the premise that "seeing is believing." Now we turn this around. Believing is seeing. Focus on ideas and thoughts that feel good and desirable, no matter what is currently happening in the external world. Instead of chasing goals or forcing ourselves in any direction, we decide instead to become enjoyably fixated on what we want to the extent that the voices of what we do not want are first honored and then muted. These are the skills which must be brought into the desert landscape of perceived powerlessness.

Whatever exists currently cannot be uncreated, but new situations, experiences, and outcomes are possible. In the past, we might have trained ourselves to comply passively, or to try to "fix" the situation when we experienced something that did not feel good to us. These behaviors are ineffective and we can choose to discontinue them. The most empowering thing we can do is to settle back down in our body, imagine a new and more appealing situation, allow excitement to build, and open our hearts to this new possibility.

We hold ourselves responsible for creating an exciting life through imagining enjoyable outcomes. With deliberate intent and love of self, we begin to dwell on positive outcomes by seeing and feeling the self successfully and joyfully living the results. Past problems are set aside, and the future is not our concern. Instead, in this present moment, we imagine what we want as if we were living the outcome right now. These exciting ideas breathe life and flow the rain of magnetism needed to bring new growth into the desert. We make new decisions about seeing ourselves as we would like to be, living a great and glorious imagined reality, doing the things we would like to be doing, and having what we want to have. We fuel those decisions with imagination. Then, much to our amazement, we feel the warmth of personal power flowing strongly in our veins as we realize we *are* capable of giving birth to higher potentials!

Personal Power Changes the World

Contrary to what I once decided to believe in my early years, we are not trapped here on Earth, we are not here to suffer, nor are we mistakenly dropped off on the wrong planet. Instead, we live on a magnificent planet where it is possible to turn dreams, hopes, and desires into physical reality. Any one of us can imagine a new invention, new way of living, or a new way of feeling, and bring those inner dreams to life. Imagine–an idea can become real! However, until we understand the concept of joining spirit-based energy with physicality, and until we personally master that ability, we often feel quite disempowered.

Your highest potential is your ability to understand that you are the creator of your life. You are powerful beyond your comprehension to consciously create and manifest your desires. Evolving into the person who understands how this spirit-physical connection works, and then gaining command over this ability is your number one task.

Reaching your highest potential can be quite a daunting task to achieve because first you must embark on a journey to clear your own physical, mental, and emotional bodies of everything that says you do not have the power or ability to have what you want. If you are asking yourself, "Why isn't my life the way I want it to be?" then congratulations! You are on your way to discovering that challenges are not what you believe them to be. Challenges are the journey you take to experience for yourself how creation works in a physical reality.

Many of us are ready to feel good again. We have coped as best

as possible with sadness, inner pain, a sense of emptiness, or depression, but it is long enough. We are ready to be finished with feeling numb, addicted, or drugged on antidepressants and sleeping pills. This readiness to take responsibility for your own well-being and joy is an essential step on the journey of personal evolution. This is the beginning realization that your life matters, your dreams matter, and you are willing to risk discovering whether, or not, you hold the power to make those dreams come true.

This process of creating change is essential to personal empowerment and personal evolution. The ability to turn your dreams and desires into something tangibly solid is an essential step on your journey to discovering your purpose for being alive. First, we deal with narrower personal desires, such as eliminating addictions, or creating health, happiness, and abundance. Once those needs are met, we naturally take another step and expand our vision into the larger world.

This decision to embark on a personal journey to feel good, to feel more alive, and live a radiant life is important for humanity. Our purpose is to share and expand love with all life on this incredible Earth, but first we must end the struggles within. Empowerment begins as we allow our own balance and enlightenment. We can create effective change in the world around us only when the change first occurs within.

We must know we are capable and worthy of personal power, of our individual ability to bring our desires into the world, before we can share this truth with others. Preaching words of peace, goodness, and love is nice, but the necessity is first to create an individual world of greater love, inner peace, and empowerment before it can exude outward.

Individual empowerment inspires the world. If you hold dear to you the vision of world peace and harmony, your current lifework is to be become the person who exemplifies such a life. You must first find yourself deserving of giving yourself these gifts before you can inspire another person to activate their personal power. You must first comprehend abundance before you can move forward and share this experience with others. You must intimately allow self-healing to occur in your own body before you can spread the truth of our ability to self-heal to others. As much as we would wish to share advice and understandings, we cannot share with anyone what we have not first given to ourselves.

A loving world begins with a party of one. It begins by form-ing a loving relationship with your body, desires, feelings, and ideas. Your inner dreams are the joy of life, the salvation of earth, and the future of the people of this planet. Often we wish to give the dream to others first. We have it backwards. Our first priority is to bring our dreams into our own lives

first. We take the time to ensure we are the ones balanced, enlightened, and joyful. Your highest potential is the ability to engage your spirit in the loving, joy-filled process of creation, turning ideas into physical matter. Achieving a personally beautiful life is your number one task.

Some may say, "How can we be so selfish to take care of our own needs when there is hunger in the world? How can we be abundant and joyful when there is poverty, war, and catastrophe?" Feeling good, wanting to be alive, and thriving as a radiant human being has to be accomplished first in one individual body, mind, and spirit before we are able to share it with others. We serve others when we become living, breathing, walking examples of magnificent lives. We move others to greatness when we ourselves have come to realize that happiness, success, abundance, empowerment, and joy are possible.

Others may have it easier because we will hold the understanding of how to allow this higher vision into physical expression. What one creates so can another create because a blueprint exists. Thomas Edison followed his inner dreams and put excitement as well as effort into the creation of the light bulb. He enthusiastically expended thousands of creative hours on his invention. Now it is easy for someone else to create a light bulb because he paved the way.

 34

As we create newly empowered lives for ourselves, we create the potential for others to achieve this same ability more easily for themselves. From this new perspective, we notice that peace and empowerment are not created by warring against that which seems unjust, but by expanding the peace that we find so appealing. War is not our solution. Fighting war does not end war. There is another way, a magnificent yet challenging way to live our own vision. We first decide to form a partnership between our mind and spirit. Realizing joy and peace come from the inside, we accept responsibility and decide we are worthy of expanding these feelings in our own physical body. Then we connect our inner joy to a goal and take inspired action to bring a joyful tangible creation into the world. Because of our actions, greater peace now exists in the world.

Zen teacher and author Charlotte Joko Beck stated, "You cannot avoid paradise. You can only avoid seeing it." Put forth effort to end your own suffering. The individual path is to release all that is oppressive and self-limiting within. If peace and harmony are your calling, you are the one who has chosen to go through the hard work of releasing the old burdens and baggage of the past. You have decided to go through the important, yet difficult, work of accepting joy, excitement, and feeling good in a physical body. Your path is

the often solitary and nonconformist path of unconditional love, even though you may be uncertain as to how to do this, whether it is even possible, or if it even matters. Your path is not to push, or use power over yourself or others in order to have what you want, but to teach yourself how to use the power of spirit to turn ideas into real life experiences.

As we find the courage to expand love in our own body, we become the carriers of a new torch. Others will join and carry the torch because one person had the courage to walk through all the darkened aspects of their being, bringing the self into an original, excited, lightened body. We want to bring the world peace. We want people to stop oppressing one another. We want people to have more power in their lives. First, we undergo the journey in our own lives.

Boredom: An Invitation to a Magnificent Life

"Life is okay, but I'm bored with it all. I get up, go through my morning habits, and keep going. During the day, I smile, engage in friendly conversations, and attend to the requirements of my work. After work, it is home to watch television, eat, and sleep. In between, there are movies, gym, music, and shopping. My days are predictable and routine. What is joy? What is excitement? I think I'm missing the meaning of my life."

If you ever find yourself dealing with unbearable boredom, treat it not as an undesirable invader, but celebrate the arrival of an important messenger. Without boredom, we would comfortably vegetate in neutral, passing time by doing the same things in the same ways over and over again. Boredom's appearance is a glorious sign of impending growth. New interests, passions, talents, or strengths seek expression. It is a wake-up call indicating a readiness for more self-love, self-leadership, self-expression, pleasure, passion, and spontaneity.

Boredom is an invitation to allow an old self to fade away and a new potential self to emerge. Certain facets of self-control and repetitive behaviors are ready to be released in favor of expanded imagination, creativity, inspiration, and free-spiritedness. What was once an effective, useful routine has now become stagnant, stale, and passive. Boredom is the interim period, a place neither here nor there. On one side sits the safe, comfortable, dependable, and yet outgrown past. On the other side sits an intriguing, daring, more passionate future. Boredom identifies the natural resistance we all have toward letting go of the known and entering the unknown.

"Boredom is rage spread thin," Paul Tillich, theologian, advises. What is this rage? For many of us, it stems from decisions made long ago in some faraway place when we determined that our dreams were not important, or that passionate self-expression was unacceptable. Boredom is a healthy sign and an appropriate emotion to life denied.

We tolerate boredom because we are afraid to answer the call to growth. Well-known routines and habits lead our lives, suppressing all that would be intimately joyful or spontaneous. We are safe in our life routine, but our inner spirit intensifies as a natural course of life. Boredom is the body telling us that we are missing a natural desire for continued growth, expansion, and creation. We are not meant to remain sealed within our comfort circles. It works for a while, but soon we feel the urge to explore new possibilities.

Once boredom reveals its presence, several options are available. We can sink deeper into passivity and dullness, seek greater levels of entertainment, distractions, and diversions to temporarily conceal the physical edginess, or we can sedate the boredom with food, drink, or addiction choices.

Another alternative exists, and that is to embrace the message of boredom. Beneath the uncomfortable discontentment lies a natural, inherent call to the lifelong process of individuation. It is time to broaden personal horizons beyond former levels of conformity and social adaptation. Greater individuality, desire, love, and expression beckon from within. A readiness is brewing to connect more deeply with the heart of our existence.

Slipping from the chains of boredom becomes easier by welcoming ideas that spark the imagination and expand the heart. What is truly important? What fascinates and engages our spirit? We have the ability to go inside, sort through some ideas, and decide what an exciting life would look like. We feel good, and our bodies feel good, when we assume responsibility for choosing to focus on stimulating desires, personal interests, and inner passions. We gently allow for the emergence of new potentials and new possibilities, and we decide to feel good in the process.

Instead of letting life just happen, we can go inside and ask, "What do I want?" Typically, the first answers contain only details about what is not wanted. Accept this as an excellent starting point. Our next responsibility is to make sure we take the extra step and actually find an exciting vision to focus on. We become what we imagine, and it is up to us to determine what thoughts and visions to activate. We take control of our lives as we spend more time with ideas that increase excitement and less with those that decrease excitement.

Will an exciting life happen spontaneously just because we shift attention from boredom to passionate visions? Obviously, the answer is no. Some individuals will wonder how in the world they can possibly imagine exciting outcomes when they are currently just barely getting through the day. They do not have a clue what to imagine; they are frustrated and mad at themselves for being in this position. For anyone, creating a larger life requires effort, patience, and time. Yet not much changes without first engaging imagination.

Who you are matters. What excites you matters. The irritation of boredom simply reminds you that energy is swirling about without passionate direction or purpose. Rather than permitting a life without meaning, victims of circumstance, imagination can set the foundation for direction and purpose in life. Boredom is an indication of a certain readiness to become increasingly loyal to internal passions, desires, and values. You can decide you are worthy of forming enthusiastic relationships with what you care about. The next time you are perpetually bored realize the beautiful magic wishing to unfold. You have received an invitation to investigate new and exciting potentials and possibilities.

The Path of Greater Joy

Where are our dreams? They lie tucked beneath old notions of conformity, oppression, and suppression. To rediscover these dreams is important, and yet it involves change. We want to feel good, to feel joy, and empowerment, but few people are prepared to go through the upheaval that change inevitably delivers. Change involves letting go of the wounds of the past and letting go of the old ways of maintaining control. Change shatters the illusion of who we thought we were. In the transition of change, there is typically fear and a host of other emotions including anxiety, sadness, discouragement, hopelessness, or worry. Change is frightening. Change is unknown. Change leads us to feel uncomfortable, uncertain, and unsettled. It is easy to see why change can be so difficult.

True change is never effortless. While we cannot bypass this intense process, we can pass through it more assuredly if we bring excitement to the playing field. If boredom is the invitation to a magnificent life, then excitement is the energy required to free the spirit. Excitement is the only emotion strong enough to overcome intense emotional resistance to change. Excitement helps uncover dreams while it builds momentum and is the element that moves us toward unfolding potential.

Excitement does not necessarily mean jumping up and down, all giddy and giggling, but it could be if that expression feels right in the moment. It does not mean hooting and hollering at sporting events, although that is great entertainment for those interested. The excitement we are talking about is the kind of energy needed to focus on inner ideas until they gain substance. Excitement is then needed to sustain the effort required to allow expression of inner concepts. Living with enthusiasm is not the same as driving to reach goals; it means living in *harmony* with the passions, desires, and values that lie within. Excitement involves noticing the ideas that bring greater life, and then feeding those ideas with daily loving attention until the time is right to take action.

How do we become happier or more joyful? For me, I initially thought that removing layers of pain would eventually reveal happiness. The idea was that if I could eliminate the layers of my pain, then ultimately joy would remain. After years of working on my pain, after years of working through the layers, I realize that as long as I continued to focus on emotional pain, I continued to find more. There was always some insecurity, lack of confidence, heartache, or sorrow to explore. One day, I had finally had enough of the process of peeling off layer after layer. Enough was enough. I was exhausted by my efforts, and yet I still had not found the holy grail of inner peace. In a moment of absolute surrender, I fell to my knees. There had to be more than feeling better some of the time. There had to be more than the painful process of going through the layers. There had to be something more, but I was not finding it at the bottom of any sad emotion. If searching was all I could do, I was ready to call it quits. I would not keep "working" on myself, or holding the promise of joy with my clients, if feeling somewhat better was the only outcome.

Once again, the answer I was seeking did not come instantly in a blinding flash of wisdom, but rather answers always come when we are relaxed and open to receiving them. In moments of humility we give up struggling, accept the situation, accept that we do not know what to do, and ask the universe directly for what we need.

My clue came unexpectedly about a week or so after my moment of surrender. I had scheduled myself to receive a massage from a respected, well-educated massage therapist. After the massage began, his energy flowed in his work and with my body, and he spoke some vital words, "Each body has a pain tract." He went on to explain that his intention was to locate this pain pathway and find a way to release the tension held in it.

With spine-tingling clarity, I heard the wisdom inside me through the words of an excited source say, "Annette, you know that if there is a pain pathway, there must also be a joy pathway." That was it! In that moment, I realized I too had been focusing solely on releasing the emotional tension within myself and with other people. I had assumed that if enough pain was released and enough layers removed, then the remaining core would be joy. What I had failed to understand was that releasing tension was not the same as building up joy.

Suddenly I shifted into a possibility that I had never seen before! I understood there was a pathway to joy; clearing out the pain, although useful, was not the same as allowing happiness. The answer seemed so simple. Allow more joy to fill my body. Yet, even with this new awareness, knowing something is not the same as becoming the embodiment of the understanding.

Increasing joy "a little" is possible for everyone. Jumping to a higher level of joy than you are used to feeling is harder than you ever imagined. However, never let anyone tell you that your ability to increase your long-term happiness is limited by your genetic set point. You truly are capable of achieving a higher sustainable level of happiness. However, understand that for everyone and not just you, the ability to step up to a higher level of joy and feel good is an effortful process, requiring much dedication. Yet, it is the most important potential of your lifetime!

chapter two

When Mind Rules over Body and Spirit

L ife is a glorious and ongo-ing journey of expansion. In other words, we have an infinite capacity to create new experiences and situations for ourselves, and this journey of change is never complete. As long as we are alive, we will desire an increase in one or more areas of our lives. We may want an increase in prosperity, health, love, inner peace, or personal success. The exciting revelation is that the act of deliberately creating change is how joy expands. It expands as we discover that we ourselves are actually capable of creating change. We grasp how powerful we really are as we learn how to focus on passionate desires, align ourselves with feeling good, and allow ourselves to receive what is wanted. With each successful outcome, a veil lifts a bit more and we comprehend the enormity of our truth that anything we desire is possible.

We possess the incredible ability to bring into existence something that has never before existed in our own lives. It does not matter if our personal starting point is extreme poverty, childhood abuse, illness, the depths of depression, or beneath a pile of addictions. We have within ourselves the potentiality to create whatever we desire and from whatever the entrance point may be. This ability to imagine a better future and transform scarcity into abundance is equal in all people. What is unequal from individual to individual is what we *believe* about our ability to create positive outcomes, our *worthiness* to receive our desire, and particularly how much *joy* we connect with the process of generating new outcomes.

From the moment a new longing or wish is born inside to the moment our desire materializes, joy is the necessary companion allowing an endless avalanche of abundance into our lives. Joy is the commitment to every moment of life, an outpouring of the heart and spirit embracing our personal desire. From start to finish, joy is the enthusiasm to live our desire passionately to the exclusion of all else. Joy cannot result from outcomes, or from merely achieving the goal. Joy evolves from the *process* of engaging in the creation of new desired outcomes.

Joy is not a logical concept, but a physical experience. For example, a form of joy, inner peace, is often experienced while praying, during a meditation practice, quietly watching a sunset, or in a moment of simple stillness. When we are playing, laughing, or even dancing, joy appears spontaneously. Great pleasure fills us when we engage in stimulating or exciting endeavors. We "forget" ourselves and have a good time. In other words, we lose the tight control we have over ourselves, soften our bodies, breathe more deeply, and remain absorbed in the current moment. The task at hand is learning to bring this type of playful joy to our desires as we walk the entire path of creating something new.

Imagine the physical body divided into three separate regions: a head region (head and neck), a chest region (shoulders and arm, chest, heart, and upper ribs), and a torso region (solar plexus, gut area, lower back, hips, and legs). The head region includes our logical intellect and verbal self-expression. The chest region contains the heart energy of compassion, spirit, empowerment, and the ability to receive and share. The torso region involves dreams and desires, intuition and passion, life force energy, and our connection to the Earth and all things physical. Joy appears as harmony is established between these three centers.

For most of us, the head region has become the dominant leader of our lives. The mind, since it speaks to us in language, is the aspect of the body to which we tend to pay the

most attention. However, the mind was never meant to be the sole source of guiding information. A life led mainly from the mind is a life out of balance. Expanding joy involves living within the entire body, with a unified stream of thinking, feeling, sensing, and expressing.

Gut level passions, heartfelt spirit, and supportive beliefs all join together in a collaborative team effort to enrich our lives. Our bodies have specific and important functions in all areas, and our responsibility is to realign, rebalance, and reorganize ourselves into a state of harmony. Personal dreams are not found in our minds. Our dreams and the power to bring these dreams to life are contained within our physical core. Increasing joy involves a decision to look past the mind, learn from our experiences, and then spend time with new ideas that we find stimulating and worthy.

Despite all the conformity we have taught ourselves to do, the greatest desire of any human is to become more excited about being alive. This means offering no apologies for ourselves and living without fear of our own individuality or self-expression. Expanding into life in a joyful manner is a systematic process, requiring patience. It does not happen by itself and it does not happen overnight. It can take some practice to remember to slow down, breathe, relax, soften our hearts to ourselves, and pay attention to our additional bodily sources of wisdom.

With minds so fully in control, it takes a bit of determined core leadership to politely but firmly ask the mind to step aside as we breathe and find value in getting in touch with our physicality and spirituality.

Mind Body Balance

The mind serves a very important purpose as a memory bank that stores and retrieves information, experiences, and impressions. It has the significant job to interpret and explain reality in organized, fixed concepts. The mind judges and compares, creates stereotypes, and prefers to deal with routine. The mind holds records of our past abilities and inabilities as well as successful and unsuccessful responses. Based on the beliefs that we hold, the mind regulates the body and controls the allowed amount of permissible joy, individuality, and spontaneity.

The logical mind speaks in thoughts and words that are easy to hear, and we readily believe all it says. However, there is a huge problem with relying solely on the mind. The mind honors all fixed beliefs about who we are and what we can do, and the beliefs we constructed. Many of these beliefs were generated primarily between the ages of zero to seven. The mind creates a concept about the world and ourselves based on

these beliefs, and then continues to maintain this unchanging perception. All current incoming information is filtered or distorted to match, and maintain, the logical mind's concept of who we were at a younger age. Trouble arises when beliefs are not updated. We remain limited versions of ourselves.

The mind is like a storage drawer of filed information. As we encounter a current challenge or problem, we look into the storage drawer for an answer. Difficulty occurs because it is not always appropriate to go into the past for a present day solution. Current problems or challenges are exactly that because we do not presently have the answer. When faced with a situation we do not know how to solve, we may become overwhelmed, angered, or collapse into helplessness or hopelessness. We may experience ourselves stressed and anxious, or teary and sad. This emotional reaction is accompanied by a strong belief. "I can't have what I want." What we fail to recognize is that we went into the mind to search for an answer that was never stored there. The mind can only "work" on the problem. It can only reach into stored information and pull out past experiences and outcomes. It can never actually come up with a new, creative solution. To develop new solutions, we are going to have to go beyond the mind to seek the answer.

The mind contains millions of previously formed concepts. Let us look at an example involving food. Suppose you ate canned spinach in 1995, and it tasted horrible. Naturally, you had a strong physical and emotional reaction. The mind combined the sensory information with the emotional response and formed an entire concept involving how spinach looks, how it smells, how it feels in your mouth, how it tastes, and how you felt when you first tasted it. A complete mental construct of spinach was born and generalized to include all spinach: fresh spinach, sautéed spinach, spinach salad, spinach lasagna. When you become aware of spinach in any form, the brain searches the mental files and pulls out the original spinach memory. Unless something happens to alter that concept, years later you will automatically shudder with disgust and say, "I hate spinach." Through experience combined with a physical reaction, you formed a belief that the mind now upholds as a mental opinion and you no longer check to see if it is currently true.

The mind's ability to form fixed concepts and to filter information is amazing. If the mind could not do this, we would have to relearn everything each day. Due to the mind's ability to form patterns, we can walk up to anything with the basic form of a chair and recognize it as a chair. It does not have to look like the original chair since it can be red or blue, leather or wood, recliner or kitchen stool. We look at a chair and automatically extrapolate previous information from the past to know this is a chair.

While this is a useful ability, it is also amazing how tightly we hold onto concepts without questioning if they are true for us now. We do not need to question our mental concept of a chair, but what about all those beliefs we hold about our power, our inner worth, or our ability to create exciting, abundant lives? We regain the balance between the mind and body when we remember to challenge beliefs that feel limiting, oppressive, or undesired. We can become aware of a belief, accept that it is real for us right now, and ask ourselves if we wish for it to continue being real. All beliefs are changeable and not quite as fixed as our mind would convince us.

The body provides sensory information relevant to now. It is in the body where we feel love, experience excitement, or enjoy a moment. If you ate canned spinach in 1995 and it did not taste good, it most likely meant your body was speaking to you in a nonverbal way, explaining that canned spinach was rejected in that moment. Canned spinach was not a food you required, physically desired, or found agreeable at that time for whatever reason. It does not mean your body would never again want spinach, require spinach, or love it in some other form or on another day. Body sensory information and an emotion provided the original spinach data that the mind stored and maintained for you.

Typically, once data is stored, we live by it and no longer check to see if our belief is still true. We take for granted that if we have a belief it must be true. We act on our beliefs without question. Unless we actually eat some spinach periodically, we never know what is true in the present moment. If someone asks you today if you like spinach now, you will form an instant negative response from your logical brain. In order to overcome this automatic, logical way of life, we need to honor the mind's verbal message, ask it to step aside for a moment, and allow ourselves to choose another sensory experience. We can feel the question with our senses by tuning in to the physical body. "Is there a possibility my physical body wants spinach now? Hot or cold? As a salad or a steamed vegetable? Fresh or canned?" We run the choices through not only our minds, but also through our physical senses.

If the mind is left to rule life automatically, without checking in with the body or spirit to determine current reality, the patterns never change and our lives never expand; we live in a stagnant world of fixed beliefs about our abilities and ourselves. This is not such a big deal as it relates to spinach, but if we look at the larger picture, we might begin to wonder, "What do I actually believe about life, about myself, or about my abilities? How do these beliefs expand or confine me?"

From Surviving to Thriving

We start life with limited brain development, using immature logic to make sense of the world. During our early development, we believe ourselves to be the cause of external events; we think we are the reason parents are doing whatever it is they are doing, and we decide we are the reason we are not receiving and sharing love in the way we want. Every child requires acceptance, validation, and love, and most children will readily conform and adapt to meet their basic needs. In this conforming stage, we decide what aspects of ourselves do not get the desired responses from other people, and are therefore unacceptable. We hide those aspects and begin to create a mind concept of who we are. This mind concept is often called our "ego."

The mind's concept of who we are is a fixed and elaborate abstraction. It is a *story* about who you are, but it is detached from the full authenticity of who you are. The mind develops this story based on various invented strategies, ideas, and actions used in order to survive. This invented story of self is supposed to be the acceptable, loveable, and likeable one, and it is the part of self that is supposed to be able to control the outside world and the people in it to give to us what is needed. "Unacceptable" aspects of self are hidden as we create "acceptable" versions of ourselves. The reality was that we

were not the cause of external events. Things just happened. Our parents had life stressors, emotions, and coping strategies unrelated to us. The world around us was already happening before we got here.

Based on our experiences, thoughts, and actual outcomes of certain actions, the mind develops a concept of who we are. This fixed "self-organizing principle" is established to provide a stable sense of who we are so that we can function in the world. Once the mind forms these fixed and stable concepts, it holds onto them. The strength of the mind lies exactly in this ability to create enduring, unchanging concepts to help us to navigate the world.

For example, imagine that you are nine years old and excited at the possibility of joining the school choir. You go to the class, stand with the other students and with your heart wide open you begin your singing audition. At the end of the song, the teacher selects you to perform a solo. Your heart is pounding with anticipation and your emotions are overflowing. The music starts and you give it your all. Suddenly, the teacher stops you, and in front of everyone informs you it was as she suspected . . . your voice was the one that was out of harmony. In an instant, your elation turns to deep shame for being isolated and then publicly rejected.

If you were already formulating a belief about your unacceptability, or a belief that exposing your self is unsafe, this humiliating experience might just be the final nail in the coffin of self-expression. The experience confirms what you had been suspecting all along: something is wrong with who you are. Because of this highly emotional encounter, all kinds of previously incubating beliefs are now solidified. Those beliefs may include not only that you should never again sing in public, but that people are unsafe, people are out to hurt you, the world is a painful place to live, you should not get too excited because something bad will happen next, etc.

In order to avoid feeling the emotional pain of shame, you decide you need to hide certain aspects of yourself so no one else will see them. Maybe you decide to hide the part of yourself that held the ability to communicate freely, the part of yourself that was joyful, or the part of yourself that was an independent risk taker. Once your beliefs are solidified, you allow your mind to take over the job of making sure these parts of you stay hidden. Most likely, you will forget about the painful incident, but your beliefs now live within you. If you ever get close to singing, public speaking, becoming a bit too joyful, or taking a risk, your mind will serve to protect you by automatically generating thoughts and actions that line up with your beliefs.

Based on your beliefs, the mind forms a fixed concept of who you are and what thoughts and actions will keep you safe. We are convinced that listening to our fears and limitations, and following our strategies for behavior, are the only ways to survive. The mind's ability to create fixed concepts can be a detriment if we live our lives solely from this information alone. This is because the mental self-concept of who you are becomes quite isolated from additional aspects of self. The problem with this heavy reliance on the mind is that we grow up. Maybe our beliefs and strategies worked well for our particular family or school environment. Yet, when we take our beliefs and strategies out into a larger world, we find that they do not seem to work so well with other people.

The mind serves us in our belief that other people have the power to make us feel good. We believe that other people have the ability to give love or to take it away. We believe they hold the joy, love, acceptance, or validation that we require. Since these are essential energies for life, we readily decide to conform, or to suppress certain aspects of ourselves so that we can get what we need from other people. We restrain certain aspects of ourselves so that we may be pleasing to others and in response they will give us happiness, love, and empowerment.

Once we allow the mind to be in charge of our life, it thrives

on the power of domination and control. It cares only about itself and lacks any capacity for empathy, compassion, generosity, or love. Why? Those qualities come from the heart, and we no longer allow our mind to connect with the heart. The disconnected mind becomes barren of passion, creative solutions, and authentic self-expression.

As we mature, we have an obligation to ourselves to move beyond surviving into an authentic life. Untapped personal power and happiness are available if we can combine the mind with the other aspects of ourselves. A strong personality or ego is good, since it means we have a strong sense of ourselves in the world. We do not need to banish or destroy the ego. However, we can reshape it by taking the time to create new beliefs about ourselves and to restore the natural balance between thinking, feeling, and sensing. Without this update and balance, we continue to live our lives under the belief that other people have the power, acceptance, love, or validation we require.

The mind is merely a limited system of getting what we want. Because of our convictions about love, it believes there is only so much power and love in the world, and its goal is to get some of it. The disconnected mind falsely believes that what we want lies outside of ourselves. Based on our beliefs, the mind also now establishes "rules" on how much power we are allowed, and how much we can take from other people. The stronger ego tries to take all available power from other egos, running over all with anger, manipulation, coercion, or other control strategies to get what it wants. Weaker egos developed childhood strategies to get power and love from others in more covert manners, such as being overly nice and cooperative, attempting to rescue others, developing illness, or playing the perpetual victim.

The disconnected mind or ego attempts to get acceptance, validation, love, money, security, and most desires from other people. It does not include the inner wisdom of what is heartfelt; but instead, it thinks about what the right thing to do is, going back and forth and round and round, trying to logically make it all work out just right. Living life based on the mind alone means we ignore the inner powers of creativity, gut intelligence, inner knowingness, or intuition and, therefore, cannot follow what is right for us in this moment. An isolated mind serves our belief that others have what we want. Therefore, it is essential to live our life playing small, laying low, anticipating what others expect, maximizing our appearance for them, or pleasing them.

A cut off mind does not imagine a better world. It does not sit down and say, "All right, this is the situation I am in. What would be a more exciting situation? What would feel even bet-

ter than this to me? What could I be imagining to bring more life and more joy to my life? What preferred outcome could I create?" Lacking connection with inner dreams, wisdom, and intuition, the mind only sees the current situation, and then tries to fix it based on strategies and beliefs formed in the past.

The sad part of this drama is that, no matter how much another person gives, we are the only ones who can heal our own self-disconnection. If we believe aspects of ourselves are unacceptable, the belief will not go away because another person found us momentarily acceptable. We will just need another fix when that one runs out. It is too late for another person to give us what we wanted in the developmental scheme of things. The time for that was in our early formative years, when we made important decisions about ourselves, learning the empowerment of ourselves, our right to have our desires, our ability to love life, and our right to self-expression. It is our job as adults to become aware of limiting beliefs in whatever form they may take, and go through the steps to form new beliefs and connect mind, body, and spirit.

Why is this so difficult? The mind's wisdom speaks to us in words and automatic actions. We are smart, we are intelligent, and we can convince ourselves of just about anything. Listening to the part of us that speaks in words is much easier than

taking time to sit, breathe, and feel the other intelligences within us that have no words. Our habit has been to remain on the consciousness level of the mind, a level that is a stagnant and fabricated story of who we are and what is available to us. It takes decisive effort to recognize the mind only contains an "idea" of self, an edited and carefully scripted story of self. To live a more prosperous life, a more joyful life, a more empowered life, we must decide it is well worth the effort to reconnect mind to bodily intelligence and to spirit.

Can it be done? Yes! Is it easy? Not really. The concept of love, spirit, and power coming from within boggles the disconnected mind that has learned other strategies. It remembers, claiming, "Hey, you weren't so powerful and loved before you developed me, and you won't be successful without me in charge." People choose the difficult path of learning to reconnect thinking, feeling, and sensing because it is the natural evolution of each person. Life becomes amazing when we re-establish a supportive team between our body, passions, and spirit. We experience the freedom to live a more joyful life, to fill ourselves with enough life energy to create the things we like, and to share empowerment and love with those around us. While the path may be a challenge, no other path is as fulfilling!

Beliefs Create Reality

As children, we generated many of our core beliefs. They were formed during a time when approval from others, acceptance, and conformity were necessary objectives. We have since grown into adults, but some of our core beliefs remain suspended in childhood states, controlling the way we currently live life. Once we form beliefs, they remain unchanged unless we actively go about the business of deciding to believe something else.

Beliefs define our identity. Yet, the truth of who we believe ourselves to be is only as solid as our determination to hold onto this belief. We can recognize ourselves as attractive, successful, determined, creative, and worthy of all abundance earth and spirit has to offer, or our beliefs can be the deepest obstacle to successfully achieving the life we want. Our beliefs affect how we act in every situation, what is said and done, and how we feel about ourselves, others, and life in general. These dated, often rigid, belief systems define our reality. They define how we perceive ourselves, how we relate to ourselves, and how we interrelate with others. The beliefs we hold determine our success or failure in everything. Embodied beliefs contain decisions about how safe we are in the world, how lovable, deserving, and worthy we are, what we can and cannot be, and what levels of passion are acceptable.

Many core beliefs lie deeply buried in our subconscious and typically run on autopilot. Seldom do we even consciously know what our beliefs are, but we can observe our surroundings and quickly notice how everything in our reality is a reflection of what we believe. We see the world through the eyes of our beliefs, and the world reflects our beliefs back to us.

Contemplate for a moment what you really think about who you are. What do you believe when you see your image in a mirror? What dialogue goes through your head when you fail, when someone refuses your requests, or when you make a mistake? Do you feel good in your body, trust your body, and live in your body? Do you love life? Is the world a safe and friendly place to live? Are people kind and friendly, or out to get you in some way? Does money flow easily? Why or why not? Are you supposed to work hard to succeed? Are you able to determine what you want and have enough energy to make it happen? Is it fun to create dreams, or are goals pursued with drudgery? Who decides? Are you generally happy and optimistic, or fearful and depressed? Who determines how you feel in your body?

The answers are clues to individual belief systems, and all belief systems are subject to change. There are no limits to what we believe about ourselves except the limits we accept and impose on ourselves. We create the world around us by

our beliefs, for better or for worse. If we have accepted an idea of inferiority concerning our attributes, or our ability to be successful or powerful, we need to be aware of these ideas. It is a belief and a truth only as long as we hold onto it, and yet a painfully limiting belief is just as powerful as any other belief.

Beliefs are opinions, preconceptions, bias, concepts, and attitudes through which we filter all life's experiences. Once we form beliefs, we hold these beliefs as true, without question. Many of our beliefs provide us with support and benefits. In some areas of life, we encourage ourselves along the way, finding humor in our journey, and generating excitement for our desires. However, a number of core concepts limit happiness and result in self-defeating actions, procrastination, abuse, or poverty.

Sometimes we carry beliefs of unworthiness. This is often characterized by a sense of being inadequate to the situation in some way, a perception that we may not have what we want, that our best is not good enough, or that no matter what we do, things remain hopeless. A sense of feeling separate from others, separate from life, not belonging, or not deserving to have what is wanted pervades. Generally, there is an underlying sense that something is basically and fundamentally wrong with me as a person, and I deserve the pain and suffering I am

experiencing. It is someone else's responsibility to take away the pain or provide the happiness sought. The unworthiness belief can take many forms, but some of the self-defeating statements can include:

* Something is wrong with me.
* I cannot.
* It is too hard.
* I am stupid.
* I am no good at this.
* If I cannot get what I want, I will be miserable.
* It is hopeless. I am hopeless.
* This is not fair. I should not be experiencing this.
* I hate this.
* This is too much work.
* Who I am is not enough.
* What I do is not good enough.
* Having what I want causes another person pain.
* I do not belong.
* I cannot do anything right.
* I am not important.
* My needs do not matter.
* Why do I have to do this?

Inner beliefs of unworthiness and insecurity keep people locked within a small comfort circle. They perceive themselves as safe from harm and failure, but they are not very alive. Inner dreams receive little attention, and energy is often unavailable for the necessary action steps required toward creating a more exciting life. If a person with unworthiness beliefs were to take action, these beliefs rise to the surface of awareness. They are like scary monsters with one purpose that is to frighten us back into our comfort box. They are not evil, just beliefs we have put into place so we could be safe. The beliefs have never been updated, so they do not know the external situation has changed, or that we now want an expanded comfort circle. The beliefs are just doing their job, doing exactly what we originally intended them to do, and they will do that until we create new beliefs. There is no point in fighting them or thinking of them as the enemy.

Beliefs of Limitation

Why is it that some people persevere through almost any experience while others are prone to despair and defeat? Are these inspirational people special exceptions we can only admire from afar, or do we all have the capacity to be joyful and alive despite our life situations? In a Zen-like and possibly metaphorical story, young Asian elephants are trained by being chained with strong iron shackles. Rage as they will, they cannot break free from the heavy chain. They learn that escape is not possible. Months later, when the elephant no longer puts up a struggle, a heavy rope replaces the chain. The elephant continues in its attempts to break free, but with far less intensity, and the rope holds. Only a light rope is required to restrain the grown adult elephant, as the elephant no longer attempts escape.

Again we ask, what makes one person prone to finding the meaning in life challenges while another becomes depressed and hopeless? Most children learn in some way to be helpless and to defer to authority figures. When children are in a harmful or painful position from which there is no possibility of escape, they develop deeper self-limiting beliefs. The harm may be in the form of physical punishment or abuse, emotional suppression, or domination and oppression of individual spirit. It is not the negative aspects of the environment that cause the deepest problems, but it is whether or not the children believe they have the capacity to assert themselves. If no assertion seems possible, their minds develop a belief in their own powerlessness. There is no longer any incentive to create different outcomes or to continue trying to improve

the situation. "What's the use, nothing I do matters." This is the thought pattern that develops. Not seeing themselves as able to bring about a positive change for the future, they give up envisioning a better future. Without the ability to envision, there is no longer the activation of personal life force or expansion of spirit toward a worthy goal. Without this activation, life holds little meaning. Apathy and submission to the situation prevail, along with despair and depression.

These children have not learned the important lessons of resilience; everyone has difficulties, everyone finds their own way through these challenges, and this too shall pass. Instead, they incorporated a belief of having no individual power to affect change. These children grow up and carry their beliefs with them. The beliefs remain below the surface and tend not to emerge until stress occurs. When faced with a challenge, old beliefs of powerlessness arise as they look to others to take leadership, fall helpless to disappointing circumstances or events, or reject constructive new ideas. Childhood beliefs of an inability to create change rise up when the need for self-supportive action is most essential.

If we believe we are unable to do something, then we cannot do it because we no longer attempt to do it. Like the elephant, we have come to accept the element of inescapability. We believe we cannot change the situation, at least individually.

Our minds may frantically and obsessively look at a thousand different options to create change in the situation, but if we have learned helplessness, then we will feel trapped. All of the options seem pointless. What needs to be done will take much effort, and if we believe our efforts will not work anyway, why bother? These helpless feelings drain the energy necessary to take action. Inaction proves the belief true.

There is no logical way out of our messy situation. Why? The mind utilizes information, resources, actions, and beliefs about ourselves based on our history. Logical intelligence contains beliefs of helplessness created by a disillusioned child. We can achieve no more than our highest belief. Albert Einstein stated, "No problem can be solved from the same level of consciousness that created it." Meaning, in part, that our mind can only play with the problem, but it cannot come up with a solution. Solutions exist on a level of consciousness greater than the mind alone. Solutions exist on the consciousness levels of imagination, excitement, and spirit. We have to elevate our processes to the adult, heart, and spiritual levels where we can once again claim our power to be effective agents of creation.

Let us imagine a whimsical analogy and compare the mind to a jar full of colored marbles. Each marble is an option for a previous experience combined with the outcome. To solve

a problem from the mind, we need to rummage through the existing marbles and pick the one that best applies to the current situation. What happens when the solution sought doesn't yet exist in our mind, or if the problem being faced is a problem never faced before? The marble we are looking for does not exist yet in the jar, just as the solution sought does not exist within the confines of the mind. If we learned patterns of helplessness, the marble we pull out of the jar as a possible solution is also loaded with assumptions about the problem itself, negative beliefs about our ability to effect change, and projections about our inability to achieve success in the future. This marble does not expect anything to change in the miserable situation and contains the belief that good things, no matter how much hoped for, will not happen.

The solution to the problem lies beyond the jar of marbles contained in the mind. The solution lies within the imagination, within the heart, spirit, and creative self. Einstein suggested approaching problems by opening up to new ways of thinking, redefining original ideas about the problem, and continually considering alternatives. This requires going past the comfort level of known solutions and past limiting beliefs about our ability to achieve the objective. This involves pushing through the emotions of the current belief system to discover for ourselves that beyond the mind is the human spirit with its innate capacity to learn, evolve, and create new and imaginative solutions.

Generating New Beliefs

Everything we believe about ourselves is changeable! Astonishingly, our thoughts, including the critical or negative ones, are nothing more than a repetitive tape based on beliefs we formed about ourselves. It is possible, even probable, that what we believe about ourselves may be inaccurate reflections of our true capacity, and yet we accept them without question. Our beliefs are not necessarily truths; we simply act as if they are our truths. Once a limiting belief system is in place, we attempt to prove to the world that the belief is false, while continually proving to ourselves that it is true. The mind automatically filters out or dismisses any counter evidence as it carefully holds on to anything that supports the belief. Old beliefs do not melt away on their own initiative, and new beliefs do not automatically put themselves into place.

Belief systems are subject to change simply by questioning them. When we are not happy with reality, we can question by asking, "Why does this keep happening to me? What do I believe about myself, the world, or others that would create this recurring situation?" We typically do not ask these types of questions because our beliefs are often painful. In asking ourselves what we believe, we invite the stinging emotions that accompany our reasons for our beliefs.

What also surprises us is the fact that because we internally believed something to be true, it has already manifested itself externally. When we ask the question, "Is what I believe true?" we look into our world and see physical evidence of its accuracy. The mind tells us, "What I believe must be true." What is not understood is the correct order of things. We believe something and *then* it is reflected in our outer life, not the other way around. We may not consciously realize how we are creating our life, but that does not change the fact that, as individuals, we create life from our beliefs.

Beliefs themselves exist within the body, embedded and stored in our tissues, muscles, cells, and perhaps even in our DNA. Our entire physical being has become a reflection of what we believe. Linked with these beliefs are many distressing, intense emotions. No wonder creating change is so difficult; it must occur not only in the mind, but also on the physical level, emotional level, and spiritual level.

If we grasp the concept that beliefs create reality, or even if we just find some inner curiosity to test out the theory, w recognize that creating lasting change occurs on the inside first, even before we receive evidence of our change on the outside. The reason we often fail in creating permanent change is that we try to make it happen on the outside while leaving our inner beliefs untouched. Creating change requires a willingness to face current beliefs and to travel through the uncomfortable emotions connected with those beliefs.

Creating change requires asking, "What do I want to believe?" We must then spend time in the land of gut-level desires, imagination, and the invisible realms of spirit to answer that question. Creating change requires trust because it is entirely a "believe it until you see it" game. Everything we currently believe is true. Everything we want to believe does not yet exist.

Creating change requires actively doing work on many levels, and one of those levels is the mind itself. Remember, the mind is a storage drawer that is filled with files of everything we believe about ourselves. The mind contains a story of our beliefs with everything we believe inscribed on neural circuits. As we move through life, we use the old beliefs so often that the pathways become quite efficient and strengthened. If the mind functions in isolation from the rest of the body, the story of our beliefs is our only reference for our behaviors, actions, and thoughts. The change we wish to create, the belief we wish to hold, does not yet exist.

Creating new automatic beliefs and deeply embedding them into the neural synapses of the mind takes some conscientious work. Current beliefs do not automatically step into the background. None of us will wake up one day with a mind suddenly full of positive new beliefs about ourselves. New empowered beliefs do not yet exist. The mind, on its own, will not say, "Hey, everything is going to work out. It always does. Relax, breathe, and trust yourself and the universe to provide the solution needed. Be open to amazing new possibilities."

Old beliefs cannot be changed. Fighting them, or even trying to ignore them, is useless. What we have created already exists, and for us to uncreate a thought, belief, or reality is impossible. There is no need to spend effort attempting to achieve the impossible. From a brain physiology perspective, what we currently believe already exists on a neural pathway. We do not have to delete the old pathway, or at least spend much time worrying about how to do this. However, deliberate and intentional efforts are required to establish new beliefs and place them on newly formed neural pathways.

At some point in your life, you learned a new skill, such as speaking a foreign language, typing, or riding a bicycle. You took a class or otherwise devoted time to the repetition and practice required to acquire the new skill. The skill did not magically appear on its own; you had to engage your mind, body, and spirit in the experience. Reading or studying about the new skill was not enough. Taking the easy route, or repeating an affirmation such as "I now know how to speak German" or, "I now know how to ride a bike" did not produce the ability to speak a new language or ride a bike. Instead, you first engaged desire and imagination to choose what skill you wanted to learn and focus upon. Excitement provided the fuel for motivation and the energy required to engage in necessary skill-achieving actions. Physical experience was necessary to understand how the entire concept played out. Love was necessary to engage spirit in the successful creation of the skill.

Let us pretend you successfully learned to master the new skill. Now, many years have passed without utilizing the mastered skill. Although the skill has been inactive for a long period, the neural pathway still exists, perhaps with reduced clarity of recall. Maybe you can vaguely remember how to type, but do not remember where all the letters on the keyboard are located, or you can still understand a foreign language, but forming sentences or writing the language is not possible anymore. If you actively participate in another class, the skills will quickly return because the remnants of the neural pathway are still in place. A bit of applied focus and repetition rebuilds the pathway.

From this, we know that once something is created, there

is no "uncreating" the skill. We do not have to go through some long elaborate "uncreating" process to no longer speak a second language, type, or ride a bicycle. We do not have to hate what we learned in order for it to go away. Instead, we stop activating a particular neural pathway, and we spend more time in other pursuits. As the neural pathways containing those particular skills lose some of their connections and strength, they fade into the background, but they still exist.

Many people, when they decide they want to create change, think they have to spend time eliminating the problem. The example above shows that this is not necessary. Instead, creating change entails imagining a new desired outcome, and then with excitement and love for our venture, and repetition of a sustained action, we can create neural pathways that did not formerly exist. Through effort, newly formed pathways eventually become as strong, or stronger, than the old, well-worn pathways. Getting excited about a goal and taking inspired action toward the achievement of that goal is a quick, "feel good" way to go about the process of building new beliefs and their accompanying solid, strong neural pathways. Being excited about something opens the heart and brings power into the body.

Creating a change in our core belief systems is a bit trickier than just learning a new skill, because we first need to acknowledge what beliefs we currently hold about ourselves. They tend to be subconscious, hidden, or below our conscious level of thought, and contain some big uncomfortable feelings. Change requires love of self, compassion, and comfort to manage these emotions. The development of self-leadership skills is essential to recall the bigger picture when stress occurs and allow needed rays of light to enter the physical body when times are tough. Change involves intentionally reinforcing a new belief until eventually the new neural pathway becomes at least as strong as the old one. Until this happens, new ideas and beliefs are not going to be automatic for us. Without new beliefs, new realities cannot become manifest.

What is the incentive to go through this process? Most people never question many of their beliefs and actively create a life significantly greater than the one currently being lived. This is not right or wrong. Perhaps you, however, are one of the few who quests for the possibility of an expanded life containing greater passion and joy, and the ability to make a difference. Perhaps you experience a missing sense of adventure, discovery, and enthusiasm for life. Others may reach a point where they have had enough of feeling bad, depressed, or addicted to certain substances. Still others are just plain tired of being led about by old patterns, the very repetitiousness becoming too dull to bear. Sometimes we wake up and realize we can no

longer tolerate how we speak, act, or treat others or ourselves. It may feel like it is time to grow up and become who we truly are in our hearts and souls and spirits. Whatever the reason to create change, it is generally never easy, requiring great courage to question current beliefs and to create a new consciousness.

The road into creating change is quite an amazing adventure. As with all adventures, we never find quite what we expected. The journey is never as smooth as we would have predicted. Facing our own fears, beliefs, and emotional responses requires much courage. Over time, we begin to accept the strange and unimaginable truth that we hold within ourselves the ability to create our life. We find the courage to let go of old truths and imagine new possibilities. We trade dispassionate striving for the experience of creation and expanding into an ever-evolving state of love. We make a difference in other people's lives when we first make a difference in our own. We make a significant contribution to this world each time we move through our own internal barriers and find the courage to become more joyfully alive.

Letting Go of Old Beliefs

Letting go is a mysterious process. It is the opposite of what we imagine it to be. There are no demons to excise or devils to fight, unless we want there to be. There are, however, behaviors within us that we do not understand, and powerful beliefs we would rather not face. We are afraid of these beliefs and feel victim to them. What is needed is love. Love is vital for the belief itself and the service it has provided, and love is even more important for what we are choosing to believe and create now.

Letting go comes when we finally stand in front of an inner belief, whether it is helplessness, anger, hatred, or oppression, and we say, "I may be afraid of you, but I will not let you run my life. I do not need to change you in order for me to be who I really am. I do not need you to love me, accept me, validate me, or tell me that you are sorry. I do not need to prove my worth to you. I no longer choose to hide from you, cower before you, pretend you are not there, be afraid of you, or even be threatened by you. I stand here before you with no intentions of destroying you. Instead, I stand here now, and for the first time I show you the love and light of who I am."

What we fear most lives inside of us. What is inside of us, even if it is oppressive, is an aspect of ourselves. It must be

faced, and we must show who we are to this aspect. This is often the hardest aspect of the journey, as we become who we are, even in the presence of what we fear most. What is released is the notion that we are helpless or hopeless, that we need to remain victims to this aspect, that we need this belief to change or love us, or that we need to rescue this aspect before we can stand in our joy.

As a quick illustration, imagine that every night after dinner you sit down, watch television, and eat dessert. In fact, you crave dessert and cannot imagine going a night without it. Eating something sweet is your reward for a difficult day and a way to relax and unwind from stress. It is how you love yourself and treat yourself kindly.

One day, you realize you have put on a few unwanted pounds and you decide you want to stop eating dessert at night. Nighttime rolls around and you try to resist, but you cannot. As soon as you put effort into not eating dessert, your belief pops up and says that you have to eat. It is true that you need some way to bring more sweetness into your life, and you need a way to release stress, but is it true that you are unable to exercise free will over the choices in your life? It certainly feels that way.

What has happened is that you had a genuine need for sweetness, joy, and relaxation. Not knowing how to generate those feeling states from the inside, you believed that what you wanted must come from the outside. You developed an action of delaying relaxation until the end of the day and relying on something sweet to fill your genuine need to feel good. This soon became a hard-wired automatic habit. Now, when you try to stop your habit, your belief is going to pop up and tell you that you cannot stop eating sweets at night. Why? Because attached to the belief are the uncomfortable emotions that you are powerless to feel good from the inside out.

Rather than face the emotional sadness that we believe we cannot connect to love, joy, or relaxation from the inside, what we tend to do is hate ourselves for being so weak when it comes to food. Then we assume even greater control over our bodies, use willpower to fight against ourselves, of course inadvertently making the need to eat sweets at night even more important.

To release this belief, we need to honor the intention of our belief, which in this example was the need to provide love, relax, and feel good. We then need to imagine a new way of providing these needs for ourselves. Of course, the question becomes something like, "How can I relax and feel good from the inside, when I don't believe I have the ability to do so?" Then, we need to put ourselves in a position of facing head on

the feeling of being powerless and find a way to say "no." We can say to our habit, "Thank you for helping me relax and feel good. But, no, I don't have to eat sweets right now, and 'yes' there is another way for me to feel good. Tonight I choose to breathe deeply and take myself for a walk outside."

Letting go of a belief requires two actions: an intention to do so and a loving connection to a new desired belief. We do not have to know how to let go; we just have to want to let go. First, we have to stop fighting whatever it is we want to release. The original belief is not terrible. Even if it is limiting or destructive, we created it, invited it into our lives, and had a good reason for doing so. It serves to keep some aspect of ourselves quiet, subdued, hidden, or small. It will not leave until we take responsibility and decide we can live without it. It does not remain to torture us, but it remains because, on some level, we still have a need to hold on.

Along with the desire to let go of a belief no longer wanted, we need to develop a loving connection to the idea of what is wanted instead. We put our thoughts and energy into a new vision, creating small growths of new potentials. Consider the lovely bromeliad plant. These plants belong to the pineapple family, usually with stiff leathery leaves and bright, attractive flower spikes. Bromeliads flower a single time. When the flower dies, the mother plant switches its energy into creating vegetative offsets, called pups. These pups grow, taking nourishment from the mother plant. When they reach about a third the size of the mother plant, the pups are ready to be separated. The pups will not mature and produce flowers until they are cut from the mother plant.

Achieving new dreams is similar to the growth of the bromeliad. When we were young, we created certain beliefs about ourselves and about life. Just like the original mother bromeliad, we grew and blossomed. Life was beautiful, and we lived it to the fullest extent possible. Even if there are things we would wish to change, life before the change is still worthy. Life is not something that starts once we figure it all out. Life is now. At a certain point, though, we know we have gone as far as we can with our old beliefs still intact. Old beliefs feel confining, and the time comes to shed the aspects that limit us now. Choosing to focus on a new dream or desire switches our energy from sustaining old beliefs (the original mother plant) to connecting it with new beliefs about ourselves (new baby plants). With time and loving attention, these new beliefs grow and mature, but for a while, they will still be attached to the much larger original belief.

One day the fledgling new belief grows to the point where it is ready to separate from the old. Until this happens, there is naturally going to be a conflict between the old agreement

we made with ourselves and the new agreement that is growing but has not flowered yet. The older belief still dominates, but the new belief also exists. The old belief can never flower again and eventually its energy will begin to fade, but it hangs on until it is intentionally released. It is not going away on its own. If we have reached this point in the journey, we are well aware of how rough it can be to be living with two conflicting beliefs at the same time. We feel pulled in opposite directions, emotionally, physically, and spiritually. The stress turns to suffering until eventually a decision must be made.

At this point, several choices exist. We can abandon the goal or dream, along with the associated new supportive beliefs. This allows a retreat back into the comfort of the life we knew. This is not necessarily a happy or expanding life, but a retreat into perceived safety. A second choice exists. In this option, we find we cannot let go of the dream or the new beliefs associated with the dream. At the same time, we are terrified, paralyzed, and cannot release the old belief. This choice can create a decision to just rest temporarily, stopping active work on achieving the dream briefly, but knowing that it still exists. This can be a time of putting the dream on the back burner until new energy, determination, support, or momentum is gathered. Perhaps an integration or incubation period is necessary before moving forward. For others, this choice of

putting the dream on the backburner may create increased stress and turmoil. They know the dream is there, and they punish themselves for not being able to take the steps they "should" be taking. If the suffering continues, some method is chosen that allows themselves, and their physical bodies, to feel better. The soothing may come in the form of addiction, numbness, depression, or even contemplating suicide as a way out of the stuck situation.

A third choice is to resolve the conflict by choosing to continue with the dream, to continue nourishing the new belief, *and* to release the old belief. Letting go of an old belief may not be easy. Old patterns worked well in the past. We bloomed and lived the best life possible, even if we did so with limitations or restrictions. Whatever the old life was, it was familiar and beautiful. It was because of the old life that new dreams were born with new potentials. The new life is the same you, a clone of the original plant, but with new ideas, new beliefs, and new possibilities. A new phase of life can begin as an adult who has outgrown old childhood limitations.

It takes great courage to reach the realization that the only way to continue is to nurture the new belief until the old withers and is released. This is often difficult because the old belief was a steadfast companion, even perhaps our only friend at times. You see, the belief is real. It is a blanket we

cover ourselves with, a wall we hide behind, a hardness sealing in love, and a block from keeping our originality from seeping out into the world. The belief kept the heart hardened, kept love safe, kept us silent, out of trouble, and out of harm's way. How can we possibly let go of our attachment? How will we protect ourselves? If we have survived until now, while attached to an old belief, what will happen if we let go? What will happen if we stop clinging to the past? Who will we be without our old stories?

When we reach the time for letting go, the mind has no answers of how things will turn out because we have never reached this point before. We do not know if we will be okay. It is the scariest place to be. We alone can decide if we will let go of strategies from the past. Imagine that many years ago, you found a partner with whom to spend your life. You had many hopes and dreams about the life you two would build together. After years went by, you realized that maybe your friend had his or her own agenda that no longer included the same things you wanted. All along, of course, the person told you that he or she loved you and that things would work out. You continued to go along with the story. After more years, you face the fact that there is no marriage, no home together, no increased joy, and no common goals. You reason with this person, saying that these things are important to you. Still this person says, "Just wait. Once you get your life together, once you are different, then we can get something going."

You try your best, giving all you can, working harder, being nice, and pleasing your partner. Somewhere inside you know the truth. This person does not share your dreams. No matter how nice or giving you are, the situation just is not going to change. You have been angry countless times, and you used all your arguments. No matter what, this person refuses to release you. It is so scary to look at this situation, for so much time and energy have been invested in the dream. All you wanted was for this person to allow you to grow, and to grow with you. You do not want to be alone. Having someone is better than having no one. He or she remains a companion, and does offer certain things; maybe if you tried a little harder, the person will finally see what a good person you are and join you in your dream.

Beliefs work in the same way. We have many years committed to a certain belief, so much time with this internal companion. How we long for it to love, support, and validate who we are and what we want now. This was never the belief's intention. We created or invited this belief to hold a specific job description. Its job was to keep down self-expression, to help us conform, and to offer security by being the one in charge. It really is not a bad guy, but at some point we traded a part

of ourselves for some safety, security, and companionship. It will continue doing its original job as long as we need it. It will never leave on its own. It will never change. As good as we get or as bad as we get, the belief is going to stick with us because we are in charge of our bodies and we are in control of what beliefs we hold. The belief is sticking around because, on some level, we have asked it to remain.

We never bargained that, if we started voicing our needs and desires, it would push us down, continuing to oppress us. Sure, this was its function, but it should change now. Inside we know that love always expands, so this belief should expand and change with us. We want to hate this belief; in fact, some part of us does. The bigger truth, however, and the one even more difficult to face is that we love this belief. It served us and provided some security and safety. We do not want to let it go. We wonder why it cannot grow and change as we do, but that is not possible. We cannot change something already created; we can only create and nurture something new. This old belief cannot be forced or changed into something new.

It is terrifying to let go of the past and of what we have always relied on. Choosing a new idea seems foreign and scary. We really do not want to be the responsible one to face the old belief and assertively say, "You can no longer live with me in my body. Thank you for all you have done. Thank you for stay-

ing with me for so long and for never leaving me alone. I love you so much. I wanted you to come with me as I grew. I do not know what will happen without you. I am so terrified, but I am ready to stand without you now. I have to let you go."

Are we ready to stand alone, without the original belief? What about the years we invested? Who will hold us? Who will cover us and keep us warm and safe? There are never any answers. People talk about faith and courage, but even faith may not always offer the comfort we expect. What will happen is a moment of gut-wrenching pain when we decide we are scared, we do not want to have to make this choice, and we do not really believe that we will be okay. Yet, despite our fear, we move forward anyway. We decide to walk a new path with our new beliefs.

Will we be alone when we release the old belief? Yes. We will be as alone as if we had left a life partner or had said goodbye to a friend, and we will feel the grief of letting go. This is a new and unknown phase of life. The feeling will not last forever, but as we are not yet grown up in our new belief, we may feel small and vulnerable. An appropriate analogy is the old saying about being a big fish in a small pond, then suddenly being a little fish in a big pond. At first, you were content with your allotted amount of empowerment, joy, and self-expression. You were content with your degree of ambition. You felt yourself to be important in a small place. When you set a goal, you decide you want more for yourself. But a goal, and the new beliefs required to support the achievement of that goal, take you out of your little pond. You may feel alone, scared, and displaced. However, only by releasing old fears about ourselves can we grow and expand into the person we were meant to be, and increase our level of joy.

Exactly how do we let go of a belief? Ritual can help create a tangible experience, signifying to ourselves that we have made a solid choice to let go. The ritual can be anything that feels related to the old belief. It can be a sacred trashing of the old diet books, cigarettes, or alcohol. Perhaps burying an object related to the old belief. Or writing a letter to both the old belief and to the new choice, and then burning it to send intentions up into the universe. Creating a ritual is similar to a funeral in that we acknowledge we have released something from within. We can bless the old belief for all it has done and given, and then allow the waves of fear and grief to move through our body. We can grieve and feel fear in the decision, but still know the decision has been made. The decision is solid and unwavering, and we are no longer on the fence.

Along with the intention and ritual of letting go, we can find comfort in knowing that something good must be released to make room for something new. As the waves of grief and fear pass, we can connect with the excitement of new beliefs. Remember that you have already given birth to those new beliefs. The work of establishing them is complete. Now they are young and tender and have room to spread themselves. Tend to those beliefs even as there is grieving about what has been let go. Pay tribute to how well you grew with those old beliefs, honoring yourself, your life, and your body. Breathe and feel the energy of excitement rising and flowing now that the old belief is no longer holding you down. It may feel scary, but at the same time, it is very exciting.

chapter three

The Body Temple

The primary purpose of life is joy. We ache for those words to be true. Generally, we get through life with good times and bad times, but can we be infused with joy? We want to awaken, feel passion, and remember who we are and why we are here. But how? Attached to us are the powerful tentacles of difficult childhoods, dysfunctional families, painful experiences, and sorrow. We desperately want out of the fusion with our limiting beliefs, but we feel held back with each attempt to escape.

In adulthood, we manage to stretch the beliefs, but never seem to release our bodies or minds from the influence of these beliefs. We try every tactic to get away from them, searching for just a bit more information so we might understand what is going on. Sometimes we scream to be released from our

pain and suffering, praying with all our hearts for some type of divine intervention, angry that help does not arrive. Some nights we feel very helpless, wondering, with little hope, where salvation is going to come from. We go to therapy, seek counselling, and attend one spiritual seminar after another. We put forth tremendous efforts to heal ourselves, and in many ways, those efforts themselves are healing. Why, then, will the joy not come? There is no easy explanation nor any easy formula to increase joy. To carry joy is a mysterious process, an unfolding development requiring patience, practice, and dedication. Joy is available in this lifetime. It takes time to open ourselves to it because we have so many deeply entrenched beliefs. Joy comes as we allow certain beliefs to fall away, as we speak to ourselves with kindness and compassion, and as we open our imaginations and hearts to desired potentials.

Part of feeling good involves nurturing inherent abilities, creating self-leadership skills, and updating aspects of our personalities. Living life in love and joy means being our own best friends and becoming unwavering supporters of ourselves. Our beliefs can elevate us into greatness and joy or drop us into despair. Let us consider the following monologue, "I know I should make some changes in my life. I have been ready for a long time. My finances are out of control. I should try to lose weight and get in better physical condition. I need to leave my current relationship. I need to find a new place to live, but I cannot. There is so much I need to do to improve my life, and I just cannot get started. I am not happy in my job, but I do not have enough money to leave. The relationship I am in offers some security, and I cannot face being alone forever. There is no way out. I do the best I can, and I will get through another day. What is wrong with me?"

This sounds melodramatic when it is written down, and yet who among us has not been unhappy in life, love, or money while at the same time overwhelmed with a sense of despair and helplessness at the situation? We generally have an idea of what needs to be done in the larger scheme of things, but we also sense the enormity of what it would take to change the status quo. The task ahead seems so huge and unmanageable that we feel trapped in a situation with no possible escape. Parts of ourselves want to shrink back into the safety of what is known and familiar, pretend that things are not really so bad, or hope that the situation will magically change on its own. Our beliefs encourage us to do just that. The beliefs of doubt and inadequacy seem so real that there genuinely appears to be no way out of the current chaos.

Reaching this point in our journey, we conclude that we are incapable of achieving our desire. Feeling lost in the dark land of inescapability, we pitifully ask, "Won't someone come save me from all of this? Isn't it enough to be a good person?" The desire for more life and more joy has gathered deep within our bodies, giving rise to new dreams. We can *almost* see ourselves in much more exciting life situations. Yet as desires and life energy rise, they come into conflict with strong, entrenched beliefs about the necessity of accepting the status quo and getting by. These are old beliefs about not being lovable or good enough, or beliefs about being alone on this earth, unsupported and abandoned.

Just as our life energy is ready to expand and flow in new creative directions, old illusions warn us to stay safe and urge us to use strategies that have always worked. Each time dreams and life energies rise, old beliefs kick into full alert. The mind acts like the robot in the 1960s television program, *Lost in Space*, with arms flailing about, shrieking, "Danger! Danger, Will Robinson!" The robot takes a protective attitude toward Will, alerting him to danger or threatening situations, so Will can take immediate action to protect himself.

Choosing to focus on inner desires awakens our spirits to the possibility of creating something new. Physical life energy rises to a level greater than we are used to. Sensing this increase, the mind kicks in with warnings of danger. New potentials with new levels of life energies rise from deep within ready to expand and move forward; entrenched old truths tell us

to cling to the known and lie low. The mind warns that our course of action is foolish, unsafe, stupid, and harmful. If we collapse under this conflict, the mind has done its duty. It has flailed about sufficiently and has used oppression, distrust, and fear to suppress the rise of spirit and new possibilities.

The conflict encountered at the intersection of change is difficult to experience and go through, but worthy of celebration. Something wonderful is happening, for a new desire is emerging, and new life energy is struggling to find its way to freedom. As this life energy rises, it also moves old issues to the forefront for resolution. By bringing ourselves into the conflict, we are asking ourselves to face certain individual beliefs that formerly governed our lives. We are giving ourselves the opportunity to expand beyond what we currently believe ourselves able to do.

Why does the world not provide what we need and want? Actually, the universe is providing us with what we seek, and that is what the conflict is all about. There was no conflict before we asked for something more. Happy or not, we were living contentedly in a small pond created by our beliefs. What was asked for was given. Now we are asking for something greater than we believe we have the right to have.

When we ask for something new, the potential of what we

want begins to gather. The universe does not keep our desires away from us. *We* keep our desires away from us. Imagine a desired new potential as a teakettle filled with water. We dare to place attention on a new desire and in doing so put the teakettle on the burner and turn the heat on. Just as the teakettle is about to reach a boil, we turn the heat off. In a similar way, we turn off the heat of our dreams just as they are about to reach a boil, removing focus from the new desire to return attention to old illusions. For example, as soon as our goal or dream requires more effort, persistence, or faith than we believe we have, we might collapse and say, "I can't have this, it won't work, and this is just too hard."

Yes, creating the manifestation of a new reality requires tremendous effort. It entails inner resourcefulness, opening to love, and learning to maintain intensity of focus on what you want rather than on what you currently have. You must master the tenacity to stay lovingly aligned with your desires even when evidence of success is invisible. Finally, you must decide you are worthy of receiving your desires. You are unlimited in what you can achieve, although you may be greatly limited in understanding how to go about gaining those achievements. Conscious creation is an act of divine partnership with what is wanted. What you create with love is formed with love and received with love. Through this divine relationship, the creation of your dreams erases fear-based illusions and brings a new era of transformation into the physical world.

Body Language

We have beautiful bodies that give us the ability to experience ourselves within our creations. These bodies are filled with sensation and sensory experiences that we discern as pleasurable or not pleasurable. Sensations guide us away from what is not wanted and toward what is right for us as individuals. Interpreting the language of our bodies is essential to our joy and purpose. The interesting thing about bodies is that they never lie. They always tell us whether we are honoring or dishonoring ourselves. They tell us if we are moving in the right direction, if we are fearful or trusting, or if adjustments are necessary. Bodies are an immediate and accurate source of feedback, a perfect guidance system telling us everything we need to know. They tell us when supportive and life-enhancing choices are made, what ideas and activities are enjoyable, what thoughts are encouraging, what energies feel good, and what foods and substances are agreeable in both the short- and long-term.

Learning to trust our bodies can be difficult but offers a much simpler way of living life. We can trust our bodies to know if

relationships, goals, jobs, or current lifestyles feel good. Our bodies offer instantaneous information about being open and connected to spirit or closed to this connection. A short cut to feeling good and creating a fulfilling life involves going beyond the need to analyze or live in the logical world of assumptions, interpretations, judgments, or conclusions.

Our bodies feel good when life energy is flowing freely. They strive to be in a state of balance, relaxation, and flow. Imagine the joy of the mind, body, and spirit working as one, all on the same page and operating in harmony from the same desire. Our bodies can only tell us when this is not happening by sending physical messages such as tightness, tension, or unease of some sort. They inform with physical sensations when life energy and love are not flowing as freely as is possible. Our bodies speak of what is amiss. They cannot change what is wrong; they can only indicate what is going on.

If the gut is all wound up in a knot, for example, the body is attempting to share important information about negative judgments preventing creative flow. It would be of great benefit not to make the feeling go away, not to fix the problem, but to breathe deeply, accept the current feeling, and relax. Open the heart to what is going on and receive the gut level wisdom held within the knot. Allow the body to re-establish flow by breathing and letting go. The body already knows how to balance itself if we release control.

The body is not a foreign object that has the power to do things to us. The body is our home, a place where we have stored our beliefs. If the body hurts, it is because we have beliefs that we should be holding back life energy, holding down gut level truths, or holding in honest self-expression. We only become aware of these physical tensions when we have outgrown certain beliefs. Our body lets us know where our beliefs live, and where they constrict our life, joy, or self-expression.

It is by your feelings that you know what is occurring for you. You may choose to push down awareness of the knot in your stomach, but it eventually becomes a stronger feeling as it knocks louder in an increased effort to gain attention. As the feeling gets stronger, the habit may be to choose a stronger action to push the feeling down, such as eating, drinking, or engaging in other avoidance strategies. If avoided for enough time, eventually an illness will form in that region. Not because the body is punishing you for not listening, but because the tension required to inhibit flow begins to wear out the body. Through our beliefs, we stopped the natural flow of individual ideas, honesty, creativity, passion, expression, love, speech, or life force. A clear flow of mind, self, and spirit are somehow not lined up as they are meant to be.

Alignment with who we are is a day-to-day, moment-to-moment process, bringing ourselves consistently into balance with a place of well-being. We can allow new ideas to come to us, saying, "I can create what I want. I want to create in this reality. I want to see what is possible in this reality." We can decide to play with new ideas and new beliefs, trusting ourselves to line up with ideas and emotions that feel good and supportive. We can open up any possibility that is exciting, and let our bodies be channels of excitement. We can take the time to nurture these feelings by spending time imagining desired outcomes, being more supportive of feeling good, and opening our hearts to these new ideas.

Gut-Level Communication

We speak to ourselves in a variety of ways. The mind transmits information through language, using words and thoughts, but the body also provides a constant source of information, speaking to us through feelings and physical senses. We are constantly providing ourselves physical, nonverbal clues about what is real for us.

We are mostly aware of our mind's verbal communication, and barely aware, or even distrustful, of the body's nonverbal

communication. Understanding nonverbal communication requires a healthy dose of curiosity and is different for each person. Every heaviness, tension, tightness, or constriction is sending important information. Complicating matters, there is no dictionary of "body language" to provide the necessary interpretation. As unique individuals, we must consciously become aware of our own body's nonverbal messages. We must continually ask, "What am I telling myself when I do this with my body?"

Did you know that the body actually has two brains? There is the familiar one located within the skull and a lesser known, but vitally important one, located in the gut. This "second brain," known as the enteric nervous system, is located in the digestive organs, including the esophagus, stomach, small intestine, and large intestine. The gut brain holds over one hundred million nerve cells, more than in our spinal cord, along with neurons and neurotransmitters just like those found in the skull brain. The gut brain has the ability to act independently, learn, remember, and produce gut-level feelings.

It also seems the two brains are interconnected, and when one gets upset, the other does, too. It is because of the second brain in the gut that we get cramps when stressed, "butterflies" before an important event, or a "gut-level" sense of whether someone is friend or foe. The gut brain does not think or analyze like the upper brain, but it is an important repository for good and bad feelings. It also handles the energies of personal power, passion, integrity, self-discipline, vitality, and confidence. Paying attention to gut-level feelings guides us in our power to choose what is right for us, realign with pleasurable ideas and actions, and create new beliefs about what is possible.

Often, because of young childhood experiences, we teach ourselves to constrict the abdomen and tighten the diaphragm, essentially cutting ourselves off from access to bodily wisdom, creative potential, and inner wisdom. Breathing becomes high and shallow, allowing ourselves to create life from survival strategies of the mind. There is nothing wrong with this, but the result is living as a limited version of ourselves. We no longer imagine a new, exciting, potential outcome, but cope with distress utilizing one of our formerly developed logical strategies. I do not know about anyone else, but I know my childhood strategies were not that empowering because they were based on fear and conformity.

Time has moved forward, and we find ourselves living in a completely different environment with different people. By now, however, the mind has taken charge. Gut-level wisdom is still available, although there may be little motivation to retrieve it. If we were shy, withdrawn, or encountered harsh criticism,

abuse, or a lack of encouragement and support as children, there is little desire to extend our inner truth into the outside world. Lacking a sense of worthiness or belief in personal power, there is little contact with gut-level intelligence.

In everyday life, we have an expression when we hear from our intuition, and we say, "I had a gut feeling." A gut feeling refers to a sense of knowing something from within ourselves. Instinctively, we know that when these intuitions arise, we would be wise to listen. Not acting upon gut feelings often leads to regrettable choices. In our gut, we know when something brings satisfaction, or when something is not quite right. If we are unable to respect our inner level of truth, we experience a gut-level sinking or aching feeling. The gut constantly speaks in its own nonverbal language, reminding us to stay true to ideas, choices, and actions that keep us in harmony with our own values.

We feel truth in our gut, but easily allow our minds to talk us into and out of things all the time. We fail to consult deep inner wisdom when we determine a course of action. We are actively, although subconsciously, engaged in keeping ourselves disconnected from authentic contact with who we really are in the present moment. When the body does stir in a manner too loud to ignore, the isolated mind goes into overdrive, worrying, stressing, and turning what started out

as an important gut-level communication into something to be feared.

When we are angry with another person, we use an interesting expression when we say, "I hate your guts." This phrase essentially means to say, "I hate the very essence of who you are." In the same way, when we no longer connect with our own midsection, we hate our own guts; we hate the essence of who we are. We are afraid to allow passions and genuine expression to rise up into our consciousness. We are afraid of who or what might arise. We are afraid the world will reject or ridicule our gut-level expressions. So we hide them, trading authentic truth for the hopes of outer validation, acceptance, and approval. We trade inner riches for the promise of outer riches. Despite our best attempts of suppression, the gut brain never stops working or providing honest information. In our gut we know when it is time to become more than we have allowed ourselves to be; it is time to grow beyond our comfort circles. It is our natural state to be excited about life, authentic, and involved in meaningful pursuits.

When we live life without trust of our physical body, we live a life that bows to outer authority. Such a life is no longer spontaneous or authentic and is restricted by what we mentally believe to be true about ourselves. The pain of leading such a life leads to overwork, perfectionism, compulsive tendencies, obsessive thoughts, numbness, depression, illness, and a host of other side effects or addictions. Our passions and dreams are still totally intact: as beautiful, brilliant, and whole as on the day we were born, but are hidden away, stuffed down and contained within the body each time we refer only to our mind and no longer include our feelings and senses. When we push individual life energy, passions, desires, and truth down far enough, depression is the outcome.

"Know thyself." This quote appears in the writings of Ovid, Cicero, and Socrates. But who is this real self? Before we begin to drive ourselves crazy with intellectually wondering who the "real" self is, we must stop. Remember that the mind is not fully connected to the body's feelings and senses. Ask the mind, "Who is my 'real' self?" and we are thrust into an adventure in suffering, confusion, and chaos. There is no answer up there. The mind wants to have stable, fixed definitions and expectations of who we are. That is just what the mind does as it attempts to make sense of things. The "real" self is not so much a logical, language-based definition or stagnant stereotype as it is a natural and spontaneous choice to follow what feels good and right in every moment. The real self involves accepting life as it is, and imaging how we would wish to express ourselves within that situation. It involves accepting our first reaction to a situation, and then going

beyond the reaction to think or act in ways that bring joy.

There is a Zen story that speaks of the concept of self: Two monks were washing their bowls in the river when they noticed a scorpion drowning. One monk immediately scooped it up in his hand and set it on the bank. In the process, he was stung. He went back to washing his bowl and again the scorpion fell in. The monk saved the scorpion once more and was again stung. The other monk asked, "Friend, why do you continue to save the scorpion when you know its nature is to sting?" The monk replied, "Because to save it is my nature."

If we really want to know who we are, we stay present to our-selves in the moment. We are not here on Earth to analyze or explain our every emotion; we feel what we feel. The mind separates feelings, emotions, and experiences into good or bad. It wants to try to fix life, or fix us, so we only experience the "good" things. That is an unrealistic expectation of life. We feel joy when we feel joy, but sometimes we feel pain. We also feel anger, rage, frustration, pettiness, and a host of other emotions. Our responsibility is not to control these feelings, but to accept them as they arise. We seek the wisdom held within our emotions, and then take a moment to decide how to think, act, or speak to create more joy and meaning for ourselves. We really do not need a reason "why" we are feeling a certain way, nor do we need to develop elaborate strategies to fix those feelings; they will pass through if we allow them. If we take the time to reconnect the mind with the heart, feelings, senses, and gut intelligence, we are able to stay aligned with who we are in the moment. Instead of scurrying about trying to fix things, we can relax, accept the present situation, and focus on whatever it is we need and want. In this way, we are able to move beyond the limitations of past beliefs and create new solutions from the uniqueness and creativity of who we are.

The Frozen Body

We experience limited joy because we put our physical bodies into a somewhat frozen state, diverting and restricting our own aliveness. Certainly, if we look at our own body, we do not literally find a division of the head, chest, and torso. What we find are muscle tensions in the neck and shoulders, keeping the head functioning separately from the body. Jaws clenched tightly to prevent authentic expression. Tensions keep the heart guarded and hidden. Muscular constrictions restrict our breathing and keep us from checking in with our gut-level desires. A tight diaphragm keeps breathing shallow and high, providing greater "control" for the mind, as we allow it to

focus on strategies for becoming a better, more acceptable person.

This physical way of being has become automatic, but it is not natural. We taught ourselves how to hold ourselves intellectually high, no longer checking in regularly with the spiritual and bodily aspects of who we are. It takes quite an active assortment of constant muscular tensions to keep the mind separate from the body. So many of us feel alone and lonely in the world. The aloneness is real, since we have disconnected from our inner self. Mind, physical body, Earth, and spirit no longer link together as they were intended. As a result, life is dealt with solely on an intellectual level. We attempt to stay in control of ourselves by pushing down feelings and opinions, drowning out our inner voices, and ignoring gut feelings and intuition.

On a regular basis, check in and notice your physical body. Sense what is automatically going on. Observe without fixing anything or finding anything "wrong." Is your physical body relaxed and open, or are muscles tense, heavy, or tight? Notice where you hold your energy and attention as you encounter various situations. Sometimes we hold ourselves up high in our heads with unconsciously tightened neck muscles and shallow breathing. We speak, think, and react without checking in with ourselves.

Observe whether your heart is soft, open, and full, receiving all the love available to you, or guarded, hardened, hidden, or even numb. The state of your heart affects the power offered to desires, the love flowing in the arms, and the compassion given to your words. With your feet firmly on the ground, notice if you feel connected to the Earth's supportive energies.

Sense how alive you are in the moment, how deeply you are breathing, how freely life energy flows, and how open and full your heart is. Take the time to regularly observe yourself, and notice what is going on with your body. Consider asking yourself, "What do I believe that I would hold my body in this manner?"

The quickest path to joy is this process of physical awareness, of consciously noticing what tensions we are holding that restrict breathing, flow, and creative expression. Notice and breathe. The body is not holding onto tension because it hates us or wants to hurt us; the body is holding tension because we have asked it to. Tension is the method we have chosen to hold ourselves in, hold ourselves down, or hold ourselves back. The body is in harmony with our beliefs, responding to these inner messages. Our amazing body, our faithful servant, always honors our core beliefs.

What are the messages we have given our body? They include

directives about keeping our inner self safe and hidden, messages that love from the heart should not be allowed to unite with unique inner passions. The result is tension designed to keep inner knowingness contained and restricted, and to keep heart energy held back. This tension allows the mind to remain in control. This might have been a good survival strategy when we were young, yet the body is not meant to remain in a frozen state, with restricted, shallow breathing, hardened hearts, numerous muscular tensions, and protective layers of fat.

Our body serves our beliefs and creates a frozen or numb state, yet this is not the desired position of the body. The body is keenly aware that love, joy, life energy, dreams, desires, and spontaneity are trapped within. The energy of all that we are remains contained beneath the physical tensions, wanting expression and release. This energy of authenticity and spontaneity does not die because we have put it into isolation. As time goes by, it becomes restless, pacing back and forth behind muscular tensions. The spiritual knocking becomes louder, in effect triggering the body to increase its tenseness as it honors physically embedded beliefs.

This conflict eventually becomes physically and emotionally painful, and so it has a way of gaining our attention. The body sends signals of distress as a natural language to warn us that self-expression is inhibited. Ignored, the signals of physical distress can become quite unpleasant. Anxiety, depression, headaches, and heart, stomach, and gut ailments are but a few of the consequences of ignored or unrelieved physical tension. Unaware of how to correctly interpret this body language, we often fail to recognize that pain felt in the body is an essential communication to loosen up, let go of control, and become authentic. Instead, we strive to achieve greater control, or take pain relievers, alcohol, antidepressants, sleeping aids, or other medications to relieve the physical and emotional symptoms.

The noticeable tensions, constrictions, and tightness of stress, anxiety, or panic are the body working overtime to push down authentic expression. We developed our own beliefs of survival, embedded those beliefs in the physical body, and gave the mind control of our life. The body must now serve deeply rooted beliefs rather than our spontaneous self-expression. The body can only respond to the natural increase of inner activity with increased tension. So often, we misinterpret these tensions. The body is the vehicle of our expression. It does not want to be muscularly rigid or layered in protective fat. But it will, until its dying day, serve our beliefs and physically inform us how these beliefs inhibit flow.

The Purpose of Pain and Pleasure

We are so much more than our bodies, and at the same time, our bodies are our beloved partners, always guiding and providing vital information so we can remain true to ourselves. Through sensations of pleasure or pain, our bodies tell us if we are pursuing life in a way that brings an expansion of creativity and happiness, or a constriction. The body continuously directs us away from what is not right for us and tells us, by feeling good, when we are on the path that is aligned with our individual truth. The body brings us away from logical ideas about ourselves, and it brings us away from knee-jerk reactions to current situations. Instead, the body gives us reliable information about what is going on right now. It tells us exactly what we do not want, and how we do not want to feel. By providing this information, we can refocus on inner dreams, desires, passions, and heartfelt love for what is possible. However, we became so skilled in our early lives at suppressing and overriding feelings and emotions, that we began to mistrust our bodies. We believe our minds and what we "think" about things rather than "feeling" our experiences with things.

If pleasure is so important to being alive, why do we have pain? Simply, pain demands attention. It keeps us alive and steers us in directions that feel better. The function of pain

 116

is a warning system that something is going on in the body requiring attention. The body is a magnificent guidance system alerting us to do something different, think something different, or act in another way. Its guidance system is designed to bring us back into alignment with pleasure and exciting new potentials. It does this through the senses: feeling, seeing, hearing, tasting, smelling, and other senses we may have, such as intuiting and simply knowing.

Life includes pain on the physical, emotional, and spiritual levels. It is all designed for one purpose, and that is: to guide our attention to what does not feel good so we may take another action. Placing a hand on a hot stove quickly leads to an automatic response of removing the hand. The pain that comes after the burn allows us to keep pressure off the wound until it heals. People who develop diabetes may sustain peripheral nerve damage and, as a result, experience neuropathy, a loss of feeling in the hands, feet, and other areas of the body. This loss of sensation may lead to accidental damage because the person feels reduced or no pain. Even when wounds develop on the bottom of the feet, people with diabetes may keep walking because they do not feel pain. A few people with diabetes may also develop a condition called Charcot's joint. Due to nerve damage, the cartilage surrounding a knee joint degenerates and leads to bone fractures. Not

feeling much pain in the joint, the person is unaware of the bone fractures and continues to walk. If left unnoticed, the injury can lead to severe deformities.

It is extremely rare, but sometimes a child is born without the ability to perceive pain. This may sound like the pain-free life many people wish for, but these children live dangerous and disfigured lives. Lacking the physical ability to provide the necessary information to help guide them through the physical world, they severely injure themselves and tend to die very young. These children do not feel pain jumping off high places, for example, and will keep doing it even if a bone is broken. They may scratch out an eyeball and become blind because they do not feel pain. Nothing stops them from inflicting injury upon themselves because there is no pain. Young children do not watch where they are going because there is no incentive to do so. Without the valuable information pain provides, the body is unprotected and soon destroyed.

Physical pain is the body's way of telling us to pay attention to something. It is a loud knock on the door of our consciousness, attempting to provide immediate information that whatever we are experiencing, saying, or doing does not feel good. When we experience a situation that is out of harmony with self-love, the body responds with a physical feeling. This feeling could be tiredness, stress, anxiety, headache, a knot in

the gut, a heavy heart, or a tight diaphragm. Something is out of alignment with the truth and pleasure of who we are.

Emotional pain can involve beliefs that we can do nothing to change or affect the situation. It may also include beliefs that we should not feel pain, we should not be alone in our pain, or that the pain will never end. The emotional pain is really just the stories we have about a physical feeling. We made up stories about why pain is unfair, why we cannot feel good, why we cannot have what we want, or why we cannot receive love. The emotional stories generally involve some form of self-pity, powerlessness, hopelessness, or helplessness.

Emotional pain is an indication of a limiting belief. Emotions are not an end point, and we are not powerless to create different outcomes even if we believe ourselves to be. The pain demands our attention and invites us to challenge what we believe to be real about others, the world, or ourselves. If we can listen to the pain and understand what we currently believe to be true, then we have the required information to take two essential actions: deliberately *move away* from beliefs, reactions, responses, situations, or experiences that do not feel good, but also *move toward* what does feel good.

The philosopher Epicurus shared the wisdom, "For we recognize pleasure as the first good innate in us, and from pleasure

we begin each act of pursuit and avoidance. Life is based around pleasure, we strive to find it, and achieve happiness. Without it we have nothing to live for." If we do not understand the language of physical or emotional pain, if we believe our pain to have no value, then we have dismissed inner wisdom and personal responsibility to create a pleasurable reality.

Finding our pain pointless or irresolvable, we may choose to push down the physical discomfort and the painful emotional stories. In desperate acts to feel better, we numb our bodies' messages, suppress feelings, and stuff them down, severing a vital connection to our physical wisdom. However, suppression is not the same as cessation and the body continues to provide information. Not knowing how to alleviate the suffering from the inside, we often choose outside fixes. In a natural attempt to bring selves and bodies back into balance and feeling good, we may unintentionally create the habits of addictive cycles.

Undesired habits and addictions often begin because we feel an uncomfortable emotion. Not knowing how to ease the pain internally, we reach for an outside stimulant such as food, alcohol, drugs, sex, money, shopping, or even goals. When we bring an external source of energy into the body, we feel good momentarily, but at some point, the eating, drinking, sexual activity, or busywork must end. The external source of feeling good stops and leaves in its wake not only a sense of unresolved issues, but also a sense of guilty despair. We question, "How could I do this again?" These new feelings of disappointment, guilt, or remorse do not feel good in the body. We repeat the cycle of bringing external energy (binge eating, drink, busywork, sex, etc.) into the body to create momentary comfort or numbness. A dependency develops on the "fix" to provide pleasure, even for a limited time. The cycle quickly takes on a life of its own.

Often, people on perpetual diet cycles or those recovering from drugs or alcohol addictions fool themselves into thinking that the addiction is the problem. Certainly, the addiction or habit is a problem in itself and requires attention, but the core issue is the need to develop greater internal compassion, an expanded spirit within the physical body, and a connection to positive core beliefs about self.

We cannot cut off external sources of comfort and feeling good without cultivating the ability to feed ourselves comfort and joy from the inside. The underlying problem is not eating, or drinking, or busyness, but the lack of empowering self-leadership skills necessary to define an exciting life, generate positive energy to allow motivation, and love ourselves from our heart to take action toward creating a new life. The cycle of addiction or seeking pleasure from the outside is okay if we can understand that the underlying intention was to feel good.

There is no shame since feeling good is our intrinsic nature. The inherent purpose and design of each living human is to seek a flow of feeling good.

Even an addiction was originally meant to bring a person back into a state of feeling good. People who choose food, drink, or some other substance simply have no knowledge of how to feel better from the inside. They chose external energies because every person alive has a drive to feel better, but we often do not understand how to go about the business of making this happen. We do not understand that feeling good involves a harmonious living relationship with the body, supportive and loving beliefs, and connection with spirit. External "fixes" tend to feel good in the moment, but they do not feel good in the long run because the outside "fix" is a limited source of energy. Outside "fixes" often also come with unwanted consequences. We will feel bad until we understand how to feed ourselves with the infinite, always dependable, always available, inner joy.

Our bodies are our faithful companions, always telling us what is right and what is not right for us. They are physical systems of pure and truthful information. What is critical is not the avoidance of physical and emotional pain, but connection with it. A relationship with the pain is necessary because the pain can tell us exactly what we do not wish to experience

 122

or believe. Half of the answer of what we want is contained within the physical and emotional pain of what we do not want. Gathering this vital information requires recognition that the body is not a foreign object. It is an extension of ourselves, allowing us to have a physical experience. If we develop certain "listening" skills, we may ask of our pain, "What is it I don't want?" When we understand what is undesired, we can assertively take two important actions: we can move away from responses, reactions, situations, and experiences that do not feel good to us, while also taking the effort to move toward pleasurable and empowering experiences.

Without understanding the purpose and value of pain, creating a somewhat frozen body seems one of the few options available. The consequence is that pain locks into place without an avenue of flow. Our bodies are left with the task of holding on to things that were not meant to be held onto. We become somewhat numb, logical, going through the motions of life but not really experiencing it as fully as possible. Left in a frozen state, our beliefs never mature, and our energies are tied up in control and coping behaviors. It takes a great deal of energy to hold on, hold back, and hold down, and little remains to follow creative pursuits.

The ability to allow greater pleasure is a journey that surprisingly requires great determination. Logically, it would seem

any one of us would easily allow ourselves to feel good, but this is often not the case. We have learned to restrain our passions, sometimes deciding it is best to be quiet, to go with the flow, to hide in the background, to be like others. We withhold ourselves from love. The daily actions of our individual life show us the many ways we deny ourselves joy when it is most needed. We must learn that nothing has to be achieved before being worthy of feeling joy or any of its relatives, such as comfort, compassion, pleasure, satisfaction, or inner peace. The ability to feel joy and consciously create an excited life comes from the inside; they are not something we must earn.

Thawing Out

Physical tensions and feelings are an invitation to explore what we currently believe about ourselves, others, and life. They are an invitation to update and balance the mind with sensing, feeling, and allowing. The body speaks by leading us directly to tensions, aches, and pains that serve as barriers between the mind's ideas of survival strategies and actual inner desires. On these barriers of tensions lie the reasons and emotions of why we decided we needed barriers. The tensions are constructed of self-imposed expectations, restraints, self-control, and rejection of certain aspects of self. Behind muscular tensions lie open hearts, spontaneity of excitement and originality, individual opinions and preferences, creative ideas, and life energy. The tensions keep us disconnected from ourselves, but if we are not connected to our own selves, then we are living someone else's version of life.

A new decision to listen to the body and heart creates a painful conflict. We must first pass through what we currently believe about ourselves before we can reach the inner self. These beliefs are the scary ones that tell us not to be too alive, too passionate, too authentic, or to feel extremely unpleasant things. The beliefs embedded on the muscular tensions say, "No, you can't come out. It is not safe. You are not acceptable. The world has rules and we've already learned how to survive within those rules."

Reconnecting mind with body and spirit requires facing these beliefs head on. There is no way around them, and no way of avoiding the emotionally painful stories connected with these beliefs. The tricky part is not to succumb to the idea that there is no escape from these beliefs. Having lived with the beliefs for so long, we are afraid that the messages are real. We are afraid to be vulnerable, to show the world who we are. If we are afraid of the initial emotional response, we quickly push the feeling back down and resume the habitual body

constriction. How much pain we feel during this "waking up" period may depend on how easily we are able to accept the presence of old beliefs without getting trapped in them. We must learn to accept that certain beliefs are present and to appreciate that we must have had good reasons for putting them into place. Old beliefs must be managed, while at the same time new beliefs that speak of valuing the body and allowing excitement must be continually reinforced.

We can compare this process of waking up and living within our body to thawing out from a light freeze. Imagine you are playing outside on a cold winter day and your fingertips begin to freeze. Back inside, your fingers begin to warm up, and what was once numb now hurts a lot. You do not want to go through this pain, but you do not make a big deal out of it. It does not mean anything other than there is pain associated with bringing life and feeling back into lightly frozen fingers. You do not create emotional suffering on top of the pain by saying, "Poor me. I can never have what I want. It's not fair that I have this pain. This pain will never end. It's hopeless." We also do not go back outside and re-freeze the fingers just to avoid passing through this physical experience. Instead, we breathe, accept the pain as part of the process, and relax. Soon, the pain stops and warm, functioning, flexible fingers are back again.

We thaw ourselves in the same way. Life did not start out with tense, frozen bodies. It began with warm, soft, flexible baby bodies. The world exposed us to certain situations and eventually the energies of those situations began to affect us, just like the cold affected our fingers. We found a way to live within those inescapable childhood energies and made many decisions in response to those energies. We taught our bodies to become tense as a way of holding safe our inner truth, love, passion, excitement, or inner self-expression. The tension may be in our neck, jaws, eyes, heart, diaphragm, arms, ankles, or anywhere we decided to limit the flow of life energy and self-expression. Eventually, the pain of this repression became automatic and normal; we may have even become numb to it.

As time passes, life force and authentic expression wish to release themselves from captivity. This release may hurt as hardened layers of protection thaw and old belief systems are the first to rise to the surface. There is just no getting around emotional or physical pain when it happens. Belief systems are typically associated with complex emotions, explaining why this is not fair or why we should not feel pain. We may even believe that the pain will never end, or that we are hopeless or helpless. Belief systems are complicated, filled with many emotions, sorrows, regrets, anger, and fear. There is no

need to analyze this or figure it out, any more than we need to analyze frostbitten fingers. Gentle warmth, acceptance, patience, time, and compassion are needed as we trust the pain will pass and be replaced by new life.

A House Is Not a Home

I stood one day, naked, in front of a full-length closet mirror. I summoned my courage to look at my total body and say three simple words, "I love you." Trembling, I opened my eyes and looked at the image in the mirror. What was the image that reflected itself back at me? As if in a foreign language, my mouth sounded out those three words. Laughter welled up from deep within, a horrible laugh that took me completely by surprise. The laughter released itself so spontaneously that it took me a moment to determine what had happened. I was laughing at the absurdity of my statement. As the revelation of this truth flooded so abruptly and unexpectedly into my consciousness, I fell to the carpet, crying from the depths of my understanding. In that moment, I awakened to my own separation of love and body.

Learning to love our bodies is just the tip of the iceberg. What we are really in the process of doing is accepting our human-

 128

ity and deciding that it might be exciting to live within our bodies. We are not learning to love our bodies as we would an object, but we are learning to develop an intricate relationship between our physicality and spirituality. Bringing spirit into physical form requires choosing life, choosing to be alive in a physical body, and choosing to feel joy.

Imagine building a new house. With great care, you choose the design of the house, the tile, the paint color, and every single detail. One day the house is complete. You move in this amazingly beautiful house, but it is not yet a home. Walking through the rooms, the house feels empty, with no individual identity. Each day you stroll through the entire house, touching it, tending to it, imagining how you might bring your own life energies to it. You buy furnishings, arrange, rearrange, and return items that do not fit with the new house. Time goes by, and you paint the walls in personally chosen colors. You clean the house, vacuum the rugs, wash the floors, and hang pictures. In many ways, the house now tells you how it wishes to be decorated. Sure, it is all your stuff and your preferences, but the house also decides where the plants will grow, how furniture needs to be placed to allow flow, what walls need artwork, and which spaces need to be open. The house determines the furniture it will or will not accept. If you listen closely with all of your senses, if you work in tandem with

your house, one-by-one the rooms begin to feel comfortable and inviting.

You listen to your house, combining personal desires and preferences with the layout of the architecture. In many ways, you establish an intimate partnership, the house and yourself working together as a team. Harmony is established. Some of your favorite furniture and artwork may not be appropriate in certain areas, or even at all. Instead of hating the house, or forcing certain pieces to fit, you simply keep moving the items until you finally find where they fit, or you decide to let a particular piece go. Every day unfolds with a sense of adventure, creativity, exploration, intimacy, and passion. It takes time, but the house soaks up your energies, waking up what was once just a structure. An infusion of your creative spirit seeps into the house, not all at once, but room by room. As the rooms unite and flow, the house turns into your home.

As you share loving creativity with the house, it absorbs and reflects those feelings. If excitement, love, fun, patience, and tenderness went into the process of creating the home, then the home will emit that type of presence. The home breathes in resonance with you, lives as a partner with you, and reflects your values, beliefs, and energies. A home created and maintained with life and love responds with life and love. It keeps you safe, attracts only good into it, and even keeps itself cleaner. The home continues to evolve, expand, and flow as long as you continue to share passion, vision, creativity, and action with it.

Walk down any established neighborhood street and notice the homes. Observe how they feel, what statements they make about their inhabitants. Some homes are drab and lifeless; others are neglected, with peeling paint, barren lawns, and scraggly landscape. A few homeowners are bored and no longer share inspired creative life energy with the house. Other homes emit vitality, and they stand with worth, dignity, and pride.

So it is with human bodies. When we were born and our bodies were brand new, we felt pleasure or the absence of pleasure. Not knowing how these human forms worked, we looked to caretakers as role models to teach us how to begin the process of bringing spirit into a physical body, and how to achieve inner calmness, love, and harmony. For the first two years of life, babies are locked into their mother's energy field. They rely on this connection to teach them how to be a human filled with spirit. When a baby is upset, the little one needs his or her mother to find the pathway back into a physical/spirit/heart connection. The baby "feels" through its mother's example and learns how to be human and connect with spirit. However, not too many young parents know how to attain this balance within their own body, and are therefore unable to provide the living example for their children. Many children grow up unable to bring spirit, love, and joy into their own bodies.

Not knowing how to bring spirit into physical form, they believe that joy or love is something other people give or take from them. Children quickly develop many beliefs and strategies designed to gain the love they require. What better way to get the love needed then to become more like them? In this process of conformity, they naturally accept other people's ideas, values, energies, fears, and beliefs. That is how our bodies become crowded inside, and even quite chaotic and cluttered sometimes.

Ultimately, these are our bodies, our homes, and our temples. They are meant to contain our energies of excitement, our passion, and our unique ideas of life. Instead, they are homes that other people have decorated. Perhaps our bodies are filled with beliefs that the world is not a safe place, or that human beings cannot be trusted. Perhaps they are filled with beliefs that we are bad, unworthy, and unlovable, or maybe filled with beliefs that we should not be so powerful, unique, creative, or expressive. These messages about ourselves are reflected in our bodies, perhaps giving us a hardness around our hearts, masks instead of soft genuinely expressive faces, a certain guardedness when around others, or thick layers of protective fat under which to hide.

If we are not feeling joy in our bodies and if we are depressed or hurting, it might be time to do some major spring cleaning, if not an all-out renovation. Our bodies are communicating that we have allowed other people's ideas and values to furnish our homes, and their ideas have taken control. When we are ready, we can reclaim our homes, turning them into the sacred temple of our spirit and passions. A clearing out of old ideas and beliefs allows room for self-supporting new ones that serve to ensure an increase in feelings of aliveness, energy, and vibrancy. Just because we did not learn how to bring spirit into our physical forms during childhood does not mean that we cannot do it now. It will take effort to move past old conditioning, but the effort is well worth the expense. We deserve to trust the life and creativity of our bodies again. We can invite other people's ideas into our bodies; we can play with these ideas, but their viewpoints are visitors, not residents.

chapter four

From Healing Into Healed

We came to this beautiful earth to continuously step beyond believed limitations and to create new, expanded ways of being. By bringing desires to life, we give ourselves permission to discover who we are, and who we can become. This process of deliberately imagining and creating new outcomes, although difficult at times, is not meant to be an endless, joyless succession of dry, passionless goal setting. The time and effort involved in achieving inner desires is how we release old beliefs and allow greater pleasure and satisfaction.

The first steps toward uncovering our dreams and desires often are painful. The process may begin with introspection, soul-searching, or even therapy. It is a time to explore past trauma, abuse, or pent-up angers. We examine old burdens and emotional pain, along with the actions we took because

of them. This is an important opportunity to verbalize clearly, fully, and honestly how we hurt. We can finally cry or scream at the unfairness of it all, openly expressing emotions and allowing ourselves to be witnessed in our pain. This part of our journey allows us to understand that we have made decisions about ourselves due to a wide variety of experiences, and we have carried these decisions into adulthood. Initially we hold others accountable for our actions, pain, and suffering, and then gradually discover the importance of forgiveness. We slowly awaken to the idea that if we are to have joy, we must move beyond focusing on the problems and initiate responsibility for creating a better life. Perhaps it is time to forgive others, to forgive ourselves, and to move forward. For some, the journey through healing and forgiveness may take a few months, and for others a lifetime is not long enough.

In the end, as adults, no one can save us but ourselves. We are responsible for our own lives and happiness. At some point, the journey of "healing" must end if we wish to discover new adventures and new potentials. We get to decide, whenever we are ready, that living in the past is counterproductive. This understanding often arrives because of boredom or disillusionment with the endless healing process. We reach the end when we exhaust the available supply of healing modalities, yet inner peace remains intangible. Years on antidepressant medications have not lifted us out of pain and into joy as hoped. Endless therapy has resulted in an intellectual understanding of problems, and while understanding the why of something may have great value, the problems still exist. Where is the elusive joy, the inner peace, the sense of fullness?

No one can change the past; no one can undo past actions. What is done is done. At some point, if joy and feeling better are the desired outcome, we finally say, "Okay. I can rant, rave, and feel sorry for myself all I want. I am choosing to be done now. I accept that this is my current reality and my starting point. Now where do I want to go from here?" The bridge of healing and forgiveness is a difficult bridge to cross. Deciding to reach the end, we must give ourselves permission to step off. A new journey waits.

The next journey is quite different. It is not necessarily easier, but because of the first journey, we now have strengths and understandings that enable us to move forward into new territory. This expedition involves the ability to both expand our *spirit* and feel greater joy *physically*. As the purpose shifts from "healing" toward decided visions of creation, we initiate key guiding principles of self-responsibility, initiative, loving self-leadership, optimistic determination, and focused direction. We no longer rely on following someone else's expertise or leadership. There is no one to heal us or provide the magic easy answer. Now we hold ourselves responsible for making specific and deliberate choices, claiming exactly what we want.

In this journey, we find that playing victim or martyr has no redeeming qualities. If we are unhappy, guilt-ridden, bored, or sick, our minds still want to point the fingers of blame, but there is no one to blame. We are the creators of our own experiences. There is no one from outside or above who can save us from ourselves. We are in charge of connecting mind, body, and spirit to become more alive, passionate, loving, and creative than we were before.

Now we experiment with exploring the process of intentional creation. We learn that imagination, belief, love, and allowing are key to the joyful development of desires. As we slowly discover that we can have what we want, we realize that we no longer have to push or force ourselves into success. We understand that, amazingly, our current belief systems have created current realities; what we believe to be true is true! All change must. occur inside before the change manifests outside. Now we get to ask some mind-blowing questions: What would happen if I allowed myself, through the power of imagination and love, to believe something different? Could I create a different reality through belief alone?

This feels quite silly at first, playing games with imagination. We sit as kindergarten students in this new arena of creativity. We see what is real around us, but we play with imaginary and exciting outcomes even as we hear inner voices saying that this is ludicrous. It takes persistence and courage to say to the mind, "Okay, I hear you. I know this looks and feels ridiculous, but I am going to continue imagining this more exciting outcome anyway." Moments when we gasp "Aha!" abound as recognition dawns that we have the ability to focus on whatever we choose, any time we want, and in whatever situation we find ourselves. We find that we do not have to remain fixated in fear, stress, or worry. Pessimism, hopelessness, apathy, fear, or anxiety are not who we are; they are learned behaviors. This is a *huge* discovery.

At first, not much changes as we practice the skill of focusing on a desired outcome instead of worrying and stressing over what already exists. It is easy to become discouraged, to throw in the towel, and proclaim this venture idiotic. We may be tempted to listen to the voices of reason and quit our silly imaginings, but what if we do not? What would happen if we continued our practice of focusing on desired outcomes and bringing enjoyment into the body even before those outcomes manifest?

This is really an Alice in Wonderland type of journey. It is almost beyond our ability to comprehend. We have to dig deep and discover vast quantities of will, perseverance, and desire to unravel the mystery of how purposeful creating works. The rules change as we work *with* our desires, *with* excitement, *with* our body, and *with* spirit to bring desires to life. The act of intentionally creating preferred outcomes requires intimate partnerships, knowing what we want also wants us. It involves learning how to abandon the constant battles, stresses, and challenges of the mind, while shifting energy into maintaining loving focus on desired solutions.

This new way of achieving outcomes is generally opposite to the way we have learned how to succeed. Here, we work with love of self, love of our desires, and love of self-expression as we explore new potentials. To work with love, we must explore love. What is love, otherwise known as joy, bliss, or spirit? Is it truly available from within? If so, where is it hiding? Can we trust it enough to form connections with it, to allow it to fill our physical bodies? Do we give ourselves permission to feel greater joy than we are currently feeling, or must we sneak, hoard, or deprive ourselves of love? Do we dare allow ourselves to believe that we are eligible, worthy, and entitled to have this joy, *and then to create with it?*

Unfolding Dreams

When we dare to shift focus onto self-desires, we need great courage. Not only do we muster the bravery to declare what is important to us, but it also takes internal commitment to achieve what is wanted. We do not know ahead of time what the outcome of our efforts will be; perhaps we will succeed, and perhaps we will meet with failure. We do not know if others will support our dreams, or if they will ridicule our efforts.

Through the hardships and failed attempts, through countless times when things get complicated and overwhelming, we must decide, repeatedly, that what we want to create is important. We are the ones who must rise early, stay up late, or quit jobs to devote time to our creations. We must come face-to-face with our excuses, no matter how elaborate or legitimate sounding they are. No one will ever know the tremendous quantities of effort required to find center and courage, day after day, to stay true to bringing an inner dream to life.

Why bother? Would it not be easier to stay inside the safety of the comfort circle? Yes, of course it would be easier. But our dreams are great adventures. Our conflicts make us aware that we have desires and hopes. We begin to believe that what we want is important. We take the journey of creating change

because we decide that we would wish to experience a different reality, and that we are ready to see if we really can make it happen. These are our first steps into discovering that we have the ability to connect with spirit and bring ideas to life.

Dreams have more to do with what we discover about ourselves during the process than with what we achieve in the end. Following the passion and joy of manifesting dreams leads us into evolution. We become more than we were before: more open, loving, confident, peaceful, powerful, joyful, and comfortable in our own bodies. A dream must be expressed, but not so other people will offer money, love, or validation. The success or recognition that may come afterward is icing on the cake, but it is not the primary motivation. The purpose is to discover we are more than we believed ourselves to be. Henri Bergson (French philosopher, 1859-1941) wrote, "To exist is to change, to change is to mature, to mature is to go on creating oneself endlessly."

When we choose to create, we impregnate ourselves with a dream, and we nurture it, carry it to term, and eventually give birth to it. This entire process is how we bring our minds, bodies, and spirits together as one. In lining up with the potential of manifesting preferred outcomes, we teach ourselves how to feel good in this now moment, while creating what we want in the future.

People often say, "But I have nothing unique to say, write, paint, or express." Perhaps it is true that most things have already been expressed in one form or another, but it is also true that no one has ever expressed them in the ways you can. Henri Matisse, often regarded as the most important French painter of the 20th century, wrote, "There is nothing more difficult for a truly creative painter than to paint a rose because, before he can do so, he has first to forget all the roses that were ever painted."

Earth is the magnificent playground where inner concepts can take tangible form. Yet, expressions of new potentials require repeated efforts until one day they finally look the way you envisioned them. Any achieved outcome requires seemingly infinite effort, trial and error, and revision until it finally feels complete to the creator. The external expression one day matches the internal dream. In other words, a congruency occurs between an internal vision and an external manifestation.

The successful expression of a dream or concept is never about whether others like it, approve of it, pay money to obtain it, or even whether it is pretty. An expression is not good or bad; it simply matches our inner vision, or misses. The importance of individual expression is whether we stay true to ourselves and the process until the outer manifestation accurately reflects the inner truth. Although this process is

usually marked with hardship, which at times requires great effort, hopefully we enjoy the overall process. If we do not, no joy suddenly appears at the end of the goal, and no growth occurred.

In life, we are taught to have entire concepts within us before beginning. The creative process is "supposed" to occur as a series of sequential steps in a model. We should complete the outlines of stories before we write the pages, or have a complete business plan before beginning a new business. Indeed, there are many examples of creative individuals who held complete visions before they painted the paintings, wrote the books, composed the music, or established a new company. This process of creation is organized and so much more effective. If this is the way your current creative process works, fantastic! However, for many of us, getting used to working with our creative process involves a learning curve. We are not used to listening to our internal creative spirit, nor do we have the ability to know exactly what we want to express beforehand. Sometimes we only have concepts and ideas, but not necessarily all the details organized and arranged. It is important to begin anyway.

How exactly do you unfold your dreams, allow greater excitement, and bring your desires to fruition? The easy explanation is that you allow yourself to have a joyful experience of living your desires within your body well before they ever appear outside in the physical reality. You can decide to stop fighting against what is not wanted, or trying to figure out why things are the way they are. Acceptance is a state of truce that whatever exists already exists. Look inside and choose your preferred outcome. You can start with the truth that you do not know how to achieve what you want, but you want it anyway. Imagine merging with your preferred outcome, spending time with it, and falling in love with it even though it does not exist in tangible form yet. Choose to walk around with the vision of your lovely desire in the forefront of your mind. Create a love affair in your imagination that you feel in your body. In essence, eat, sleep, and dream the vision in ways that feel delicious in your body.

You may have no idea of exactly how you are going to achieve what you want, or how long it will take. You just know what you want, and you decide to create a relationship with it. You fill that relationship with possibility, excitement, and love, energizing your journey with fun as often as necessary and as often as possible. Nurture the expectation that what you want will happen, although not necessarily as quickly or smoothly as you would like.

 145

Sisyphus and the Rock

How many times have you set a goal, but ended up losing sight of what you wanted and in the end never accomplished it? How many times have you quit your goal? Then you blamed yourself for not saying enough affirmations, or not trying hard enough? Perhaps you even thought something is wrong with you, or that you do not deserve to have what you want.

On the other hand, there have also been times in your life when you set goals, and you actually did an excellent job of succeeding. You ended up victorious, but something about it did not feel complete. Perhaps the triumph felt hollow or even disappointing.

The desire to create change requires the inclusion of some form of excitement during the entire start to finish journey. Otherwise, your life may be filled with the anxiety and emptiness of striving to achieve something that is forever elusive. The Greek myth of Sisyphus tells the story of a man condemned to an eternity of rolling a boulder to the top of a mountain. His entire body strains with physical effort and pain as he labors to roll a block of stone up a mountain. At the very end of his effort, he achieves his purpose. Sisyphus then watches as the stone rushes back down into the lower world. He must walk back down the mountain and begin the

entire process again. This is his eternal task; his torment is the hopeless labor he must endure.

We generally do not understand that change for its own sake is *not* the real reason we set the goal to begin with. Yes, of course we want the outcome. But we want more than *just* the outcome. There is a reason beneath the reason. If we are not aware of this underlying reason, we may feel condemned to endless achieving and striving, one goal after another, but never finding the peace we so desperately seek.

The reason we seek to engage in the difficult process of change is to grow beyond a specific definition of self. Our soul's desire is to let go of a limiting belief, expand our capacity to love ourselves, feel worthy, and be in charge of our happiness. Perhaps we are ready to alter our self-concept, raise self-esteem, boost our accumulation of positive feelings, have more life energy, feel more capable, or think differently about life. In one form or another, what we really want is to raise our ability to feel good from the inside out. Not because we achieved the goal, but because we were excited about personally choosing the goal, incubating the idea, nurturing it, and being involved in the process of birthing the goal.

Unlike Sisyphus, we are not condemned to achieve one goal after another for all of eternity. However, being eternally

involved in the act of creation is our destiny. We create change in life simply because it is our essence to do so. Our spirit is creation. It seeks to bring new potentials into existence, because its nature is to expand. We complete the tasks because we chose them and because they are important to our personal evolution, not because outside influences forced them upon us. We complete the tasks to discover whether it is possible to become more than we believed ourselves to be.

At the end of the goals, we will not find that others love us more because of the labor we endured. In fact, in all likelihood, no one else will ever know the pain, courage, determination, and endless hours of effort it took to succeed in our personal endeavors. Inner voids or inner loneliness will not be filled merely because we reached the end of the goals. Our lives are not magically wonderful just because we reach the perfect body shape, have all the right answers, become the top executive of a company, or gather large wealth.

When the process of creating involves little or no joy, there is no actual point where we would ever allow ourselves to say, "Yes, this is it! I have done it! Look at what I have achieved. I now declare myself loveable, good enough, and acceptable. I am now complete!" Even though we accomplish all we want, if an inner belief tells us that we are not good enough, then we never will be. Achievements remain unrecognized while mistakes are readily criticized. The hollow feeling remains, and new goals are set immediately upon completion of existing goals. The process is relentless and exhausting since there is no end. No feat of excellence, no external tributes will gratify what we lack internally. When we find ourselves unworthy, bad, wrong, unacceptable, or when we believe that we are powerless, nothing from outside, not even our own accomplishments, will ever be enough to fill the empty holes within.

We decide to set goals because inside we are ready to see ourselves in a new light. We are saying, "Hello, this is my life. Now, where exactly do I want to be spending my time and energy? What is important to me? What do I wish to create here on Earth?" These goals are not really supposed to be passionless endeavors. For example, have you ever been around dieting people? You know the ones who are obsessively following food plans and counting calories. These are not the most fun people to be around, and quite truthfully, they tend not to like being around themselves, either. The average dieter engages in an entirely analytical process. They follow a set of rules and restrictions of what they should be doing, when they should be doing it, and how. They eat good foods and avoid bad foods, and they find themselves either good or bad based on their choices. The whole time, they are really up in their

minds, trying to fix a problem and trying to do something to their bodies, instead of working in collaborative relationship of creation with their bodies and desires.

There is nothing wrong with taking the path of dieting, for all paths lead to greater self-awareness. My aim is to suggest that goals, undertaken in this traditional analytical sense, have missed the entire point of why we set the goal to begin with. And the point is that we wanted to feel better from the inside out. The way to do this is to involve ourselves in the deliberate act of creation. Analytical goals only involve the mind. They leave out the body and the spirit. It is the entire progression of achieving the goals by aligning the mind, body, and spirit into one continuous process of creation that gives meaning to life.

Life is a constant progression of achieving the next desire, and this achieving is never complete. What becomes important is the realization that we will always be pushing stones up mountains, not because we have to, but because spirit seeks expansion. We may always choose to push the stones with anger, resentment, and expectations of rescue at the end, or accept that pushing the stones is the meaning of life. Unlike Sisyphus, we can choose exactly what stones we want to push up the mountains. In addition, we choose to utilize the type of energy that brings greater joy, empowerment, wisdom, and

love into our physical bodies during the entire process.

The world may one day celebrate the success of our outcomes, but that is not the soul reason behind our desires. The motivation is the process of self-discovery. Exactly what are we capable of doing? The answers will remain elusive until we take risks and try. Our fears are always that we will find out our original beliefs are real and that we are as powerless or worthless as we believe ourselves to be. Nonetheless, we set forth on the adventure of manifesting our desires to see for ourselves what is true and what is not true.

Our destinies are not to be ruled by past beliefs, or to feel small, insignificant, and powerless. Dreams, and the process of bringing those dreams to life, are how we continually explore, search, grow, and evolve. We dream great dreams, not to become better than others, but to explore a different expression of ourselves. We achieve, not to gain approval from others, but because we were born to allow ourselves to have new life experiences. If the rocks we are pushing come from deep within, then there is no greater pleasure than to find ourselves pushing those rocks. Joy fills us in the present moment as we push rocks that come from within our dreams and desires.

Excitement is a blessing of magnificent strength. Excitement

is the energy necessary to move our feet up the mountain, and the energy necessary to open the heart's doorway to love. It is charged with determination, and the fuel that can lead us to the ecstasy of creating our truest, most joyful life. It is the energy that drives destiny. We embrace excitement, integrate its power, magnify this force, and connect it with our deepest desires because desires not connected to excitement will seem a curse. A desire with no partnership to excitement continues to imprison us inside the rigid structures that allow no mistakes, no expansion, and no increase in empowerment, compassion, love, or joy.

As we climb, there will be great inspirational days, and there will be days that are gray, cold, and harsh. It is up to us to keep walking up the mountain, to stop for a while, or to go back down. None of the choices are right or wrong. They have always been our choices, our particular adventures. Eventually we realize that the important thing about life is how we choose. Do we back up our choices with commitment and self-love? Or do we weaken our choices with stress, insecurity, and a lack of confidence?

Don't Drown in Sorrow

The act of conscious creating is different from traditional goal setting. Creating comes from within; it is self-reliant, and filled with loving energy and desire. Strong self-leadership skills involving persistence, commitment, will, and dedication are required to bring inner visions to life. Someone has to believe that what you want is important, and that job belongs to you. While there is such a thing as beginner's luck, most people seeking to achieve something new will find themselves clumsy and often fail in the unfamiliar tasks required to attain new dreams. That is the purpose of dreams: showing you the inner strengths that you need to uncover and develop so that you can become something you were not before.

Stepping into the arena of intentional creation requires full immersion into self-appreciation. Most certainly, the process of deliberate, intentional creation of desires is sure to generate inner resistance, fear, disappointments, and failures. Along the path, watch out! Fear, procrastination, doubt, worry, frustration, hopelessness, helplessness, and extreme tiredness are going to rise up from within and question the journey. Without self-appreciation, it is easy to get lost in the difficulty and give up.

Difficulties are to be expected. While not pleasant, in the

153

end, these hurdles are necessary for you to remember how to love yourself. Your fears and emotions can teach you how to become saturated with self-appreciation and how to remain aligned with new possibilities even when the situation seems hopeless. Challenges can teach you that the way to feeling good is not reached through excessive worry and stress. Only by remembering the big picture, recalling your love for yourself, and opening your heart once more can you become a channel for all that is great.

Leading yourself through current realities into imaginary new potential realities requires surfing the edges between what is tangibly real and what is an illusionary dream. This mysterious process, this potential of having the ability to consciously create new realities, seems illogical. The concept of intentional creation through imagining new realities violates former agreements and beliefs, not to mention that our minds think we are goofballs to play around with such ideas. Plenty of beliefs and uncomfortable emotions surge through your body when you step onto this edge. Without self-appreciation, it is difficult to remain on this edge while loving yourself in your current reality and working with your available love to envision a brighter future.

Change is difficult because it necessitates leaving the comfortable and familiar world behind to explore unknown potential realities. This creates instant internal conflicts as the mind warns us that we have survived and, for the most part, prospered with the old beliefs. The known is more predictable than the unknown, and we prefer the safety and security of existing realities. The strategies of our minds are similar to the axiom, "The devil I know is better than the devil I don't know." In other words, if we stay with the familiar then we are safe and will not get hurt.

Change challenges the beliefs we hold about ourselves. It challenges individual identities and the sense of security we get from those identities. Change requires releasing something that has taken a long time to build and that has led to successful lives, replacing it with something unknown that has no proven advantage. Without compassion for self, the journey makes no sense.

Stepping into the unknown can easily knock us off balance. If you have ever been to the ocean and found yourself overcome by a giant wave, you may recall how powerful and frightening the force can be. It can catch us, lift us off our feet, and tumble us around until we do not know which way to swim for air. One moment we are playing in the beautiful ocean, and the next moment the whole world is out-of-control. Getting trapped between beliefs on the edge of an old reality and beliefs on the edge of a new reality is a little like that. One

moment we are playing with the beautiful concept of creating new potentials, and the next moment we are toppled and overcome by fearful emotions. It is not the best possible place from which to make our next choices, write our next words, or paint our next strokes. In order to move forward, we need to get out of the tumultuous emotional waves, and we need strong leadership skills to do it.

A popular Zen story tells of an old man who accidentally fell into the river rapids leading to a high and dangerous waterfall. Onlookers feared for his life. Miraculously, he came out alive and unharmed downstream at the bottom of the falls. People asked him how he managed to survive. "I accommodated myself to the water, not the water to me. Without thinking, I allowed myself to be shaped by it. Plunging into the swirl, I came out with the swirl. This is how I survived."

While the point of any Zen story is to draw our own conclusions, I see this story as suggesting that first we must accept whatever emotions or situations are currently upon us. There is no point in fighting them or attempting to stop them. Instead, we can cry, shout, or do whatever is necessary to move the energy of the emotions. We can speak the words of self-pity and unfairness, and then stop, breathe, and accommodate to the situation. Even though we are experiencing powerful emotions, it does not mean whatever we think it

means. It just means that beliefs are present along with powerful emotions, both suggesting that we cannot have what we want. In the bigger scheme of things, it is not true, but truth is that until the moment we actually release this belief, what we believe to be true is true. This is quite a paradox!

Whenever we decide to create change, we naturally dredge up unconscious beliefs and their attached emotions. As much as we do not want to feel the uncomfortable emotions of fear, doubt, insecurity, or helplessness, the underlying intention of change is to lift these limiting beliefs up and out. We cannot avoid this process, and we do not have to fight the beliefs or emotions. We need to learn to center, and then go with the flow. If we can ride it out, without drowning in huge emotions, this, too, shall pass.

At this point, multi-directed strategies are needed. Hold on tightly to imagined desires as the waves of beliefs and emotions pass. Occasionally pull out of the overwhelming emotions to see the big picture. Run to the nearest mirror and remind yourself that your dream is important. Do whatever you can to retain the idea that nothing defeats the spirit within you because nothing is more powerful than spirit. Once you remember your bigger picture and your dreams, you can pick yourself up, generate some enthusiasm once again, open your heart, and get back on your horse again. Even when you

stumble and fall, even when you are most fearful, you can remain in love with yourself and your dreams.

Leading from Center

Change needs to be led, and like it or not, you are the leader! Yet, rarely have we learned effective successful self-leadership. While some great leaders are naturally born that way, most of us have to learn the fine art of accepting personal responsibility to *identify* a meaningful direction for life, and then leading with *compassion* and *commitment* toward that destination.

Developing effective self-leadership is probably the most important work you have during your lifetime. Being involved in the creation of your dreams is not the same as harshly chasing goals. All too often individuals attempt the journey of creating change by attacking their objective with pressure, frustration, anger, or hatred. Being successful requires a different approach. Instead of trying to get rid of something, an effective self-leader puts action into expanding the feeling of what they desire. Creating a new life involves developing the capacity to hold onto your dreams with passion, despite encountering a multitude of unforeseeable challenges.

Being an effective self-leader means reaching into your depths and deciding not to suffer during your journey. Instead, you feel good loving your self for having a dream. In addition, you feel good as you nurture the positive expectation that you will have what you want. You may not be sure exactly how or when your desire will manifest, but you decide to feel good nonetheless. You will not give up until you have what you want. More importantly, you will not punish yourself during the journey just because you have not yet mastered your ability to create something new. Trust that you will learn. Trust your goal, and the obstacles it presents to you. The journey, with all of its experiences, trial, and errors will teach you how to take an idea and blend your spirituality and physicality until an outcome manifests in your life.

Most of us, at some point in our life, must assess our current self-leadership abilities, and admit weaknesses or immature strategies of the way we treat ourselves. We discover that bullying ourselves into goal achievement is ineffective leadership. Self-criticism, harsh self-judgment, and disparagement not only do not feel good, but also do not work to create lasting results. This type of domineering self-leadership involves pushing or forcing ourselves to achieve goals. We use stern and harsh tactics to remind ourselves of what we "should" be doing. Yet, the overall outcome of this type of approach is

that we become rebellious, resistant, defiant, and sometimes even helpless or hopeless since our best efforts are never good enough.

Typically, we are unaccustomed to leading ourselves through the process of goal achieving with love. Instead, we use force and power to battle and conquer what is not wanted. We traditionally set forth on missions to defeat the enemy, and crush the parts of ourselves that we despise. We push ourselves into action, thinking that if we can conquer and overpower, then victory will be ours. We wage war within ourselves and use power to force our way to success.

Aggressive behavior can work, but we receive only external victories. If we do attain a goal through this type of self-leadership, the victory is often shallow and short-lived, and we feel empty, lonely, and joyless on the inside. The goals may have been achieved, but so what? Now we are left with the goals and the strengthened "might makes right" approach, but we feel beaten down. Using force to crush anything is not a permanent solution. It merely perpetuates problems. To feel joy and empowerment requires pursuing dreams, with no sense of threat, guilt, or self-punishment.

Some of us end up being terrible self-leaders because we are such people-pleasers and have crippling needs to be loved by everyone. We often fill our days with activities unrelated to what we most want. Everyone else's needs and wants come first, with no time allocated to the pursuit of personal, heartfelt passions. Through our actions and choices, we say, "yes," when we should say, "no."

By contrast, strong self-leaders look within and determine personally meaningful desired outcomes. Desires become priority, and daily action is taken to continue movement toward a successful outcome. Internal criticism is valued and listened to, but the overall objective is not abandoned because of fear or uncertainty. Successful self-leaders allow themselves to pump their vision full of enthusiasm and expect a positive outcome. They fall in love with what they want, even while it is still in the imaginary state. An effective self-leader assumes initiative without waiting for someone else to provide direction.

Self-leaders accept responsibility for the choices they make in life. They do not get sucked into a "victim" mentality where they blame things on their past, on their parents, or on other people. They accept their current limitations and choose to grow beyond them. They show drive, optimism, determination, self-discipline, will, and flexibility. When things are going well they acknowledge their effort and reward their success. When things are going badly, instead of giving up, they study the situation and adapt their strategy. Strong self-

leaders learn to find humor in the journey, even when things are most difficult.

To sustain energy, action and progress are frequently rewarded, while excuses are plainly identified as self-sabotage. An effective self-leader is willing to take a risk, accept challenges, and assume all the consequences of failure. Failure is regarded as inevitable, and when it is experienced, a strong self-leader will compassionately carry him or herself through the disappointment and pain until they are standing on their own two feet again. Another important skill is discovering many creative ways to remember the big picture and look for the best in ourselves, especially during the worst of times. Consider for a moment your individual self-leadership style. Is your style:

- ☀ Verbally punishing and aggressive, or quietly effective and assertive

- ☀ Energetically pushy, or open to creative solutions

- ☀ Immobilized by inaction and lack of direction, or committed to daily action

- ☀ Weakened by fear and self-doubt, or strengthened with excitement and love

- ☀ Chaotic and unstructured, or steadfast and consistent in overall direction

* Punishing because your best is never good enough, or filled with celebration for your efforts and accomplishment

* Critical and self-abusive, or filled with praise and encouragement

Taking effective leadership of your own life is, perhaps more than any other factor, the key to freedom and personal power. Leadership is about knowing where you want to go in life. It is the capacity to choose a course of action from among various alternatives and summon determined purposefulness, conviction, and resolve to consistently make choices that move you forward toward your dreams. Developing effective self-leadership allows you to love who you currently are, but also to use the love you have to create a new life experience.

It is normal and common that change is difficult, and we can be quite stubborn and inflexible with ourselves at times. However, when we encounter resistance to change, we need to stop; not give up, but to reassess our leadership style. Breathe. Realize that challenges are something that we must go through, and a sign that movement in the right direction is occurring. Initially, we lack authority within certain aspects of ourselves. We give in to resistance or we bully ourselves. Instead, what we need is to develop the leadership characteristic of personal authority. Authority is not a bad word; it is not force, hatred, oppression, bullying, pushing, or shaming. Authority is the ability to know which direction is exciting, and which direction we choose to follow. It allows us to stand strong in our purpose to create change, while not backing down to fear or inner resistance.

What we want is valuable and important. In moments of doubt, it becomes essential to know how to regroup and bring mind, body, and spirit into a unified focus. It is okay that there is opposition within us. It is expected that with change some aspects of our selves will throw giant tantrums and scream, "No way!" These moments of doubt and resistance provide opportunity to incorporate new leadership skills. The mind will follow, inner aspects of ourselves will follow, if they detect solid leadership and if they know the desires are resolute. Strong internal leadership involves the capacity to take a firm stand on the objective and believe in our overall ability to achieve the outcome. We can be highly flexible with how or when the outcomes will be achieved, but the desires themselves are inflexible.

When inevitable resistance arises, there is no need to fight it, to be fearful of it, or to give in to its tantrums. We can learn to breathe, and know that we will not give up on our overall objective. If we are dedicated to our goal, then it becomes easy to listen to internal objections or resistance. Conversations can be had with those aspects of ourselves. We can understand where the objections are coming from and what we need to do to feel safe. Often, fears contain important information we can use to make goals more complete and more satisfying.

Imagine a man has dream to be a renowned and prosperous painter. He imagines he has the ability to paint so deep, so touching, that his images contain the ability to penetrate the heart, heal and transform, and bring joy to those drawn to his work. Every day, this painter spends time with his dream, bringing spirit into his body, imaging himself able to convey his spirit in paint. In the background, an objection starts to nudge at him. In time, the fear becomes louder. Rather than pretend he did not hear his fear, or rather than giving up on his dream, he takes the time to understand his fear.

In this case, he realizes he has a fear of fame, making public appearances, speaking to groups of people, and being exposed to criticism. With this information, he can go back into his original vision and add some missing aspects. The painter can go back into the vision and now imagine that he also possesses the expanded capacity and capability of being able to enjoy public appearances. The dream becomes more complete as it now incorporates being a renowned and prosperous painter who is exciting to see, and who also feels powerful,

confident, and safe in front of others, even when faced with criticism.

Respect objections and realize they often contain valuable information. A good self-leader does not change course just because there is an objection. A good leader takes a stand, assesses the objection, and finds a way to unite the mind, body, and spirit by outlining the overall objective. The desire is not up for debate, but it can be amended to include anything that would make manifesting it more joyful, more expansive, or more exciting.

As we move closer to success, critics tend to multiply and grow louder. The critics may be real people or inner aspects of our selves. We need to make peace with the fact that there will always be voices, internal or external, who criticize every decision we make; it is just our fears manifesting themselves. Realize many of those critical people or aspects of ourselves are excellent at identifying problems, but they are poor problem solvers. Strong leadership involves learning the art of listening to criticism, thanking these critics for identifying possible problems, but ultimately making decisions for the good of the desire, not simply to please the critics.

Inspired Leadership

With effective self-leadership, we consistently remind ourselves that the point of achieving any dream or desire is to feel better than we currently feel, not worse. While we will certainly encounter setbacks, challenges, and difficult days, overall it is our responsibility to ourselves to make the journey an overall affirmative experience. Purposefully aligning our thoughts and actions toward feeling more alive and impassioned during the process of creation helps keep our legs beneath us, knowing that what we want is ours to have. If our leadership style lacks excitement, we essentially cripple ourselves. We make the journey a mental pursuit of goals, rather than a full-bodied, life-enhancing experience of creation.

Deciding to create a change in your life leads to the unfolding evolution of living the life you want to life. The process of creating change leads you into new maturity from which you can live a more empowered life. Goals are amazing if you look at them from the big picture. They are not supposed to be easy. Their purpose is to allow an action process during which you decide to face your fears and make new decisions based on self-love. You decide whether to find yourself worthy, whether or not to forgive yourself, and whether you deserve to feel good in your life and body.

A goal is not a quick fix. Instead, it is a road leading inward. On this road, you discover self-worth and just how much power you have to effect change in your life. With each step, you decide whether you will risk sharing love with your goal. As you set forth with a specific goal, you are placing your feet firmly on this Earth and accepting yourself as being human, real, sovereign, and supported. You are deciding that you do indeed live here, in a body. Since this is true, you decide it is time you take charge and make your life an enjoyable experience.

The purpose of any goal is to remember that your ability to feel good comes from the inside. It is not dependent on whether you have been naughty or nice, or whether you are pretty, or rich, or even thin. You will face many challenges during your journey, and each of these provide a new opportunity to consciously recognize how you currently limit the love you give to yourself. Love is available in all moments, not just the successful ones. Love is available whether you are achieving, failing, or finding yourself in the midst of a difficult life situation. Love is not something you need to earn, and it is not a reward given at the end of a goal.

Enthusiasm is a form of self-love that is necessary to provide the energy needed to sustain action. We all occasionally welcome the support of friends and family, but accomplishing

your goals is a very personal endeavor. It is not up to anyone else to make you successful or to provide the encouragement needed to create something new. Nobody else has to think your ideas are good ideas or applaud your efforts. It is your responsibility to get excited enough about your concepts that generate the internal motivation required to move from point A to point Z. Each point along the journey is a new chance to discover the grandest miracle of life: you are God also. You discover there is nothing you or anyone else can do to keep down your inner spirit without your permission. No one, and no obstacle, has the power to defeat the divinity within you. You discover that you can learn loving self-leadership skills, create a deliberate and joyful relationship between desires and spirit, and design a great life for your self! If you merely push at goals, or think the joy you seek comes at the end of goals, you are missing the objective.

To become compassionate and expert leaders of self, we need to exercise practice, persistence, and dedication. It calls for inner commitments to dreams. We open our hearts to what is no longer wanted, grateful for its service, but at the same time, we joyously command our new choice. We confidently take a stand, and say, "I have a right to have what I want. I will not wage war against myself to have this. Even if achieving what I want takes months or years, I am going to have

this. I want this, I am excited by this, and I will persevere."

Achieving desired outcomes requires a continuing source of energy, and that energy must come from the inside. It comes from your inner spirit that brings messages of support and encouragement. Your excitement about what you want is the energy that turns dreams or desires into realities. The more enthusiastic you can get about your dream or desire, the more readily it will become manifest. This does not mean that you think positively and then one day you turn around and your outcome has magically appeared. Of course, not! Committed and sustained action are required for the expression of any idea or concept, but the doing gets done because you have chosen, not because you should. Excitement generates the energy necessary to overcome inertia and maintain the physical and mental effort necessary to achieve the desired outcome.

Inspired self-leadership leads to empowerment. And empowerment is a good thing. We all want it. We all need to know we have it in order to feel good in our bodies. In addition, empowerment brings to life ideas and concepts that are important to us. Empowerment challenges our assumptions about the way things can be. This power does not come from outside of us, it does not come at someone else's expense, or from pushing at our goals. We do not have to go into battle against anything to gain empowerment. Power expands as we learn to work with channelling excitement and love into our great and glorious imagined realities. We are creators, destined to continuously design new potentials. We are forever climbing an infinite ladder of exploration. Empowerment is the realization that there is no destination, but rather the forever process of joyfully creating new experiences and greater love.

chapter five

Become Obsessed with Feeling Good

What is the highest potential for any human being? On a day-to-day basis, we are each living our highest potential. The relationship with ourselves, our physical bodies, and others are in their highest potential. The magnitude of love, power, abundance, joy, inner peace, or passion currently embodied is the manifestation of our highest potential. On average, we have never been able to do better or live better than we are right now. We may have many grand concepts of magnificent lives on Earth, but unless we determine to reach a new higher potential, those lofty dreams remain ethereal until we bring them into physical form.

"What is my purpose here on Earth?," we often wonder to ourselves. The answer, in its simplest form, is to feel good. Feeling good happens when we align with ideas that engage our spirits, spark passion, bring more life, and open our hearts. We feel good when we are excited by the possibility of bringing an individually important dream to life. Our mission is not to save other souls or to create global peace. Other souls are not in need of saving, and not all people actually want a peaceful Earth. Our purpose is far more glorious and exalted: We are here to imagine meaningful lives and to discover that we are capable of bringing them into physical form. We came to Earth to create lives only we can imagine, to see how they play out, and to see what the outcomes are for us.

Most religions and spiritual teachings tell us that joy is an inner quality. The belief is that at the core of each person lies calm radiant joy. In other words, everyone is born inherently happy. If joy is every person's birthright, why do we all not feel joy most of the time? We have taught ourselves through much repetition to focus on things that make us feel worse. It is far more common to place attention on feeling anxious, stressed, worried, angry, sad, depressed, burned out, shut off, or numb. We may say we want to feel happy, but we actually seem to do anything we can to avoid it.

When facing challenges, the most common tendency is to struggle with the problem. We tolerate pain and discomfort, cling to worries, and dwell on unhappy thoughts. It seems normal to fixate on the problems or undesired experiences and worry about them, analyze them, kick them around, pick at them, and obsess over them. When the uncomfortable feelings become too much to bear, they are ignored or pushed down, essentially denying ourselves any bodily wisdom of what is wanted and not wanted. We make choices to dwell on what feels bad, and sometimes we attempt to move away from what feels bad, but we make very little effort to actively move toward what feels good. A lot of energy is focused on problems, but not much is directed toward what we *want*. We seem to be experts at postponing, or totally avoiding joy.

This strategy of avoiding joy does not help because solutions cannot be found by looking at the circumstances of the problem. Fixing attention on problems only makes things worse because what we focus on expands. The overemphasis of attention on problems creates additional uncomfortable feelings, which, in turn, raises stress, and our minds conjure up worst case scenarios. This stressed state of mind and body shuts down our ability to respond to a problem with wisdom, love, and creativity. When in a stressed condition, we interpret our problem as a real physical threat. Finding ourselves in a state of survival, our choices are now limited to fight, flight, or paralyzed inaction. We can drive ourselves into quite frenzied states of feeling bad because we mistakenly believe that external situations must be resolved before we can feel better.

Perfect joy is at the core of every being, and we experience joy as an internally directed, self-allowed state. There are no problems to solve first. There is no event, no person, and nothing external that can provide the state of feeling good we search for. There is nothing to accomplish, achieve, or attain before we are worthy of feeling joy. We do not have to be popular, thin, rich, good enough, nice enough, or even pretty enough to feel joy. We each simply allow or disallow joy.

The next time you are feeling something less than joyful, try the following little experiment. Acknowledge the aspect of self that is not feeling good, and then ask, "What must I believe to feel this bad?" Now, although it might take considerable effort, remove attention from what feels bad and connect with what you want to believe, what you want to imagine, and how you want to feel. At the very least, engaging in this exercise provides amusement as we see how attached we are to what is wrong, identifying who wronged us, or what is wrong with us.

The stickiness of feeling bad is quite interesting. Instead of quickly removing attention from something that feels painful, we remain there. It is like having your hand on a hot burner and not removing it. While your hand sizzles, your thoughts play with the pain, questioning whose fault it is that your hand is on the burner, how to blame and hurt that

person, or how to blame yourself for having the experience. The simplest course of action seems to be to remove your hand from the burner and instantly feel better. Curiously, it requires gathering tremendous will to lift out of the mind's ability to play with problems and move into a state of imagining better outcomes.

Not understanding the importance of loving ourselves or wishing ourselves well, we focus more on what is happening than about how to feel better. Emotional pain is an inner guidance system telling us that current beliefs, thoughts, and actions are out of alignment with love of self. Feeling bad is a big clue to make some adjustments and move on to find situations, experiences, actions, or expressions that feel better, look better, and sound better. Within the state of not feeling good, we can find the core wisdom of what we do not want. Our responsibility is to gather this wisdom, then love ourselves enough to turn our attention to what we want. Imagination allows us to dwell on preferred outcomes and to feel better, at least a little better, almost instantly.

"Nothing is more important than my self-compassion." We cannot control circumstances outside us, but we can decide what goes on inside. In each moment, we can choose what we want to imagine, and what we want to feel. If we are not imagining outcomes that create feelings of joy, we can choose again. We

always have with us the freedom to choose a higher potential.

Problems are a signal to be more creative, or to do things differently. Yet when we most need to be creative, we are often least able to be so. Therefore, the single most significant thing we will ever do to transform the situation is to find ways to stop the fear response and move into a more resourceful state of creative imagination. Ordinary people like you and I are fully capable of expanding our options. One of the most surprising things we will discover is that the universe can, and will, actually support us. The key to receiving this support is to breathe, relax, and imagine a much greater potential. The ability to lift out of stress and then imagine better outcomes makes all the difference to our situation and its solution.

Learning to become obsessed with feeling good takes time and practice. The desire to feel good, supported by our beliefs and actions, is a choice we make daily, or even hourly. We alone are responsible for creating this state. Retraining ourselves to come back to the present moment, align with inner creativity and positive expectation, instead of worrying is a gradual process. Yet it is possible to learn how to remove attention from disruption, anger, worries, and stress, and instead place focused and excited attention on new, desired outcomes. We determine how much time we spend playing in the land of feeling good or the land of feeling bad.

It may seem surprising to some people, but the human capacity for enjoyment is great. Reward areas in the brain seem to be greater than areas that produce unpleasant experiences. If this does not appear to be currently true for you, explore how to expand the pleasure experiences in your mind, body, and life. "What can I do right now, today, while I'm feeling unhappy to produce some pleasant experiences?" Look for pleasing moments. Intentionally seek occurrences of happiness. Decide to look for things that feel good. No matter where you are, no matter what you are doing, no matter what your experience, it is your dominant intent to look for what you want to see.

Training yourself to focus on feeling better is not necessarily an easy task to perform. First, you have to decide you want to feel better. Secondly, you decide that it is your responsibility to take initiative and do something for yourself to feel better. You decide that your life is valuable and meaningful, and that you are ultimately responsible for the beliefs you hold about yourself, the thoughts you dwell upon, and the actions you take or do not take. Third, you take action and do things you do not normally do. You look into your own inner creativity and ask, "What could I do right now to make today slightly better than it would be if I just let it run its natural course?" Lastly, you gather faith that your actions will reap results.

Initially, you will not create a fantastic life just because you started looking for the joy within yourself and within life. You will be sceptical and want instant results. Instead, everything starts small. However, your actions, if you persist, will be cumulative, and the joy you seek will expand with intention and practice.

Infinite potentials and infinite ways of being are available to each person. From wherever you stand, from whatever unpleasant or unhappy situations you are experiencing, other possibilities are available. However much joy is embodied within you, more is always possible. The amount of empower-ment and love available to you is capable of expansion. How-ever, alternative potentials never come to you on their own. You will not be more joyful, peaceful, or empowered until you imagine yourself to be so. The seeds of a better life can only take root if you decide to breathe, gather the wisdom of your feelings, and then utilize your imagination to focus on a happier desired outcome. In turn, your creative spirit will provide the perfect opportunity or action step needed to begin the process of making your imagined reality come true.

I hope I have done an adequate job outlining the absolute ability we possess to create change while not glossing over the actual difficulty involved in doing so. Vast joy, love, inspira-tion, and abundance are available. These experiences never magically appear at the end of the goal, but are cultivated and magnified as motivation is fueled with excitement instead of force. The process of change will naturally bring old beliefs and emotional disturbances to the surface as they prepare to release themselves. There is no way around our deepest fears. Perhaps the hardest lesson to learn is to accept the fears as they arise without falling victim to them, while constantly refocusing on more exciting outcomes.

Expanded lives do not just happen. Creation requires shifting from reliance on others to reliance on self. We advance by our own efforts, by self-motivated and self-constructed ways and means. We are the masters of our own destinies, free to shape our own evolutions. Lifting our hearts and lives into greater possibilities requires desire and effort. The power and the love within will not show themselves; they must be sought. Excitement is pivotal to bringing these energies to life within us. We can master the ability to consciously accept beliefs and emotions whenever they arise, while we also develop the capacity to empower imagination and focus on outcomes that offer radiance, delight, and brilliance.

It takes determination, but you are capable of lifting yourself out of the stickiness of feeling bad and into more exciting imagined outcomes. External situations do not have to change first for this to occur. Right now, in this moment,

you can feel good. What you are currently feeling, believing, and experiencing represent limited potentials. They are not forever experiences. Other choices are available. More power is available. Instead of simply reacting to the world and situations, you can exude love into any situation, if you first exude love into yourself.

The Myth of Feeling Good

Beliefs can be negative and self-destructive or they can be positive and helpful. The key point is that we choose what we believe. If our beliefs have created a world that now feels limiting, painful, or less than abundant, it is our responsibility to recognize we want more for ourselves and make the efforts to change. Perhaps we are thinking we do not deserve to feel better now because we do not yet have what we want. Or perhaps we refuse to think we deserve to feel good in this moment because we have tried and failed before. How self-limiting such ideas can be!

We deserve to feel good when we decide we are ready to feel good; it is not something that has to be earned. Despite the way most of us live our lives, we can feel good without being dependent on outside circumstances or on someone else. We

can feel good whenever we decide we would like to feel good, with or without completing an advanced degree, losing those ten or two hundred pounds, or getting a promotion. Life is happening right now, and it is not something that begins once goals are achieved.

In fact, feeling good now generates the excitement needed to imagine happier outcomes and allowing access to creative new solutions. Many people accept that they do not have the option to feel good until they have what they want. They argue by saying, "If I accept where I am, and I feel good about myself now, then I'll just stay here forever." That is a viable, logical concept. Of course, it is not true, but it is a good argument completely designed to keep us in our comfort zones. In truth, we are not going to be inflated or lethargic bumps on a log when we bring acceptance and love to ourselves. As human beings, we are here to perpetually create, explore new ways of living, and discover new truths. That is what keeps us alive and excited. The choice to feel good allows us to access the empowered motivational energy to take action.

Self-love is the process of sitting down and deciding what outcomes might be exciting, perhaps choosing overall dreams to guide our lives during the next week, month, or year. We could choose outcomes that would captivate our attention and engage our love. These dreams could be sources of much joy.

We do not need to push ourselves toward goals while at the same time going into battle against everything we currently have. The moment we start fighting anything, we add to the problem. If joy is the desired outcome, imagine the desired outcome filled with joy; imagine a body and life filled with joy. Imagine yourself filled with joy as you make your dream life come true. Anticipate and expect joy to enter your life and body. Sow seeds of contentment where you are now. In the fourth century BC, Socrates said, "He who is not contented with what he has would not be contented with what he would like to have." We do not need the outcomes of our dreams to validate our existence. We are already validated. For the most part, life is meant to be a pattern of personally valuable experiences to enjoy, not just to endure.

Imagine feeling joy flowing through your body. If it helps, recall playing in the warm tropical ocean and feeling very free, or remember feeling alive as the strong southern wind blew through your hair. As the memory of a joyful experience flows through your body, breathe it in and slightly magnify the joy.

As you feel physically good, also bring to mind the situation, desire, or dream you want to create. Feel joy while simultaneously imaging yourself having already attained your goal. Notice what is so exciting about having what you want.

Continue to enlist all your senses to engage more of the mind and nervous system. Smell your success, hear the sounds of your success, and allow the images of success and joy to fill your body. Live as you would like to live; feel life flowing passionately inside your body; become the exciting outcome. Let there be no separation between your life, your body, and your desire. You are your goal, and your goal is alive because your breathed life into it. Stand up in your body and put yourself in situations that please you. Do whatever it is you want to do, exactly the way you want to do it. Have engaging conversations. Compliment yourself and receive compliments. Share your joy with everyone as you adore people and they adore you.

Is this not sounding more fun than using criticism and punishment as motivation? Instead of worry, stress, and old beliefs pushing you toward certain goals, you can utilize desire, inner passion, and positive expectation to create a relationship with your goal. You can breathe life into your idea. Even though the outcome is not yet achieved, you can feel good because you know what you want, and you know in what direction your life is moving. Your current reality may be difficult, but it does not have to remain that way. You deserve to feel good, even just a little good, right now. Let your imagination play with whatever life scenarios seem constructive to you. You do

not have to focus so intently on everything that is not right. If the mind wants to keep working on the problem, fine. You can still learn to stop, breathe, relax, and find your center. From there, you can take steps to increase your ability to feel better. You do not need to retrain the mind, or stop the mind, in order to imagine a new potential.

What we focus our attention on really does grow. Aligning with new potentials utilizes new energies that never existed within us before. We are accustomed to harsh self-discipline and will-powered determination to get us anywhere, but whenever we push, something must push back. It requires taking a chance, learning to let go of control, and trusting our bodies once again, but we can choose to feel good now, even while we play with new potentials.

Imagine yourself living with extraordinary joy and abundance, with no more vast amounts of time spent obsessing about problems and no overwhelming sense of helplessness keeping you from what you want most. This peace and joy is not something you must earn, and it is not reserved only for the saintly or for certain special people. It is available to you right now. You may not be able to feel completely filled up with joy, but you do have the ability to find at least a tiny speck of it inside of you, and then breathe some life into it.

Joy is a choice you make, and when you make the choice, the universe responds. You say, "I want to feel happy." Then you imagine what feeling happy would look like to you, and feel like to you, and you allow that image and feeling to happen in your *body*. Then the universe knows what you want, and it says, "Okay." As you continue to teach yourself how to create from *within* your body and form a relationship *with* what you want, you will discover for yourself how the mystery of life works.

How much joy you feel, or how much is allowed into your body is dependent only on you. Making the choice to feel joy does not mean you open a tap and instantly your body fills with warm, unconditional love and compassion. Gut-level desires do not suddenly rise to the surface, and hearts do not immediately soften. I suppose this could happen, but that might be a bit frightening. We are accustomed to maintaining control and keeping our bodies tight. We are habituated to allowing only a limited amount of life through our physical bodies. If we allowed the fullness of joy, we might go crazy with the unfamiliar higher level of energy.

Joy is life energy. Joy is the love energy that you are. Joy is creative energy. In essence, joy is not a mental idea, but a feeling in your physical body. Currently, you are used to living with a restricted amount of life energy, love energy, and creative

energy. You would feel quite uncomfortable if you suddenly turned the tap on full blast. You would not know how to deal with all that energy.

Your self-chosen goals serve a multipurpose task. They allow you to slowly open your inner tap and physically experience slightly more life energy, love energy, and creative energy. Goals also provide an avenue of creation. In other words, you get to choose how you will work with your energy, and what you want to create. You will experience greater empowerment as you learn to work with your energy and direct it into self-chosen personally meaningful goals. Joy expands as a result of taking daily inspired action toward making your goal real. The lesson is that joy does not come after the goal. Joy is the entire process of goal achieving.

Divine Selfishness

Is self-love the greatest love of all, or is it narcissistic and indulgent? The often unspoken truth is that human beings always put their own needs first. That is the way of the world. Every belief we created, and currently live, was devised as an attempt to keep ourselves safe, protected, and have our needs met. Our personal needs guide every belief, strategy,

and action. Each belief was our best attempt to get what we needed and wanted from the world and from people. Mark Twain, the noted author, advises, "I courageously and without judgment look at the patterns I have created in my life. From his cradle to his grave, a man never does a single thing which has any first and foremost object but one—to secure peace of mind, spiritual comfort, for himself."

When we embrace the truth of self-importance, we can begin a sacred journey into understanding our divine natures, the joy possible in our lives, the beauty of the physical world, and the importance of our physical bodies. To unite ourselves with our spirit requires acceptance of individual empowerment. We must learn to realize what our needs are and assume responsibility to give ourselves the love and happy lives we desire.

Giving what we most want to others comes naturally for most people; giving ourselves what we most want is the difficult undertaking. What we often fail to realize is the reason we are so willing to give to others. Believing that love, joy, validation, safety, abundance, and acceptance come from outside, we give to others so that they will in turn give us what we want. It is a natural conclusion: if someone outside of you holds what you want, you will discover strategies and ways of acting to earn or receive that love, security, or validation.

Turning this system around is quite an undertaking. The way we have learned to live seems reverse to what is required to create a joyful, happy, or fulfilled life. Creating a meaningful life involves a journey into divine selfishness. Instead of giving away all of our love, we decide to give it to ourselves first. Instead of expecting someone else to rescue us, or provide love, safety, security, or validation, we decide we are personally responsible to making that happen for ourselves. Letting go of control, allowing ourselves to take actions and think thoughts that feel good right now, focusing on self-chosen dreams, putting steadfast and ongoing effort into the attainment of that dream, and loving ourselves during the process can involve quite an unfamiliar transition.

Deciding to create a better life for yourself requires devotion to your needs, a concern for your own interests, passions, and welfare, regardless of what others want or expect from you. You put yourself on the number one line of your daily priority list. In every journey of empowerment, personal concerns dramatically narrow down from universe, planet, countries, society, family, friends, and partner all the way back down to you living in a human body. Your life is about you. The importance of your life is about you making you happy and fulfilled.

Each journey of personal evolution requires selfish time devoted to answering, "Who am I? What do I stand for? What beliefs and ideas must I expand in order to become more in love with life and myself? What actions must I take to feel better? What would a great life look like to me? While I am alive, what pursuits are meaningful to me?" During this time of introspection, we begin to realize that choosing what feels bad over what feels good is no longer an option. Trading our values and dreams for the hopes of gaining outer approval is no longer appropriate.

Instead of saving everyone else, or saving the world, we decide to create our own version of Heaven on Earth. This happiness, this fulfilment must occur first in a very narrow place. We must learn to value ourselves to such an extent that we bring excitement and joy into our own bodies first. We decide to dig deep and remember an important dream, or we choose a meaningful goal. We make ourselves healthy, happy, and fulfilled. We create a life that is safe and secure. We create abundance.

We learn to stay focused on what we want and learn how to return easily to a place of feeling good. We learn how to connect with spirit, how to bring our spirit into our bodies, and how to unite spirit with our goals. We learn how to bring spirit into physical form, whether that form is our own body, or

whether that physical form is a business, painting, book, or some other creative expression.

You are here to create. You might ask, is this not selfish to put my desires and my needs first? It is very selfish. Yet, whose dreams would be more important than the ones you were born with? Within total divine selfishness you will discover another truth, one of divine selflessness. When you create a life and a body that overflows with joy, empowerment, and fulfilment, you overflow this potential into the world.

Just because you learn to put self first does not mean you forget everyone else in the world. The ignition of personal passion, excitement, empowerment, and creation is contagious. Expansion of self in the form of joy, creativity, money, power, or life energy, allows expansion to occur in those around you. What is allowed to flow through your own body flows through the world. What you are is what you share. Depressed people share depression, and poor people share poverty. Excited people share excitement, and empowered people share empowerment. What fun would it be to create a magnificent reality unless our friends and family were capable of creating magnificent realities, too? We do not really want to be alone in our abundance. At least I do not. I want excited, powerful, healthy, and abundant people to play with in my new realities. We cannot force those we love to give up their old ways and come with us,

but if we have the courage to create our own passionate and fulfilled lives, we are able to model this potential. Those who follow your example more easily create what you have created for yourself.

Dreams allow you to become adventurers and seekers of what is possible. In the time of divinely selfish exploration, you will encounter and release fears. These experiences allow you to re-establish body-trust. You allow love and light to illuminate aspects of self that were formerly dark. Step-by-step you bathe in the radiance of your being, and as you do so, this loving radiance becomes a part of your physical structure. You become love itself and the love of all creation. What you become flows to all beings you have shared with in the past, present, and future.

People who are elated in their everyday lives have a presence easily sensed. People feel good around people who feel good. A person who has mastered becoming a bridge between their spirit self and their physical self allows the journey to be so much easier for others who are also interested in this ability. You can only share what you are. If you have intellectual concepts of new ideas, you are capable of sharing those intellectual concepts. Logical intelligence passes from one being to another. However, if you embody a concept and manifest it into your own physical reality, you are capable of so much

more. The embodied understanding passes from the physical body of one being into the physical body of another.

For example, if you wanted to learn how to attract wealth into your world, you could learn the concepts from just about anyone who wanted to teach it. However, to really open up this gateway for yourself, would require a teacher who had already opened up that gateway for him or herself. The person who has allowed joyful abundance into his or her own life has the ability to share this potential with you. It is not that you would gain the instant ability to master wealth just by standing in their presence. Instead, you would absorb the blueprint, the possibility, of that desire from them. By being in their presence you would understand, "Oh, that is how that feels. That is how that works. I like that feeling." It is sort of like a road map transmitted from the person who had mastered the ability to you. You still have to put action and effort into creating wealth, but now you are not trying to do the impossible. You have felt, with your very own beingness, that what you want is a potential that is available for you.

Creation, or goal achieving, is an idea combined with a feeling. It is imagination combined with action. It is spirit combined with your human body. These are all different ways of saying that your life journey involves your ability to understand how to work with your spirit and create in a physical world.

 194

In the beginning, your selfish pursuit of creating a joyful and fulfilling life is narrowly focused. Everything tapers down to you and your fulfilment. As you overcome addiction and give yourself stability, as you trade poverty for abundance, or as you exchange boredom for passion, your self-fulfilment will generously begin to expand outward. Your joy and enthusiasm spreads to the people you love. Maybe not all at once, but within relatively few years, you will see how your courage to selfishly become more joyful and more empowered has affected their lives in unforeseen ways.

The truly selfish give of themselves selflessly because they have honored their own unique talents, desires, and self-expressions. They have filled themselves with love, connected their love with creative ideas, and expanded love as they brought their creative expressions out into the world. They freely share the love they are, because they realize that love is an unlimited, ever-expanding resource. They are not afraid to share their love because they now understand that no one can take it away from them. They have learned that by giving love to themselves first and continuously, their cup never runs out.

Dream New Dreams into Life

We are capable of divine creation. In this journey, we stop expecting other people to rescue us. In turn, we stop rescuing the world or hiding from the world. No longer do we need to take on other people's problems as if they were our own. No longer do we need to hide our passions from others. If other people are in pain, our hearts open fully in compassion—and yet we lovingly recognize the burden of their personal empowerment lies not within us, but within them. We assume the best and expect others to accomplish their desires and succeed in their adventures. We can relax and see the beauty in other beings and the beauty of their situations. We are all exactly where we need to be, or where we want to be, in our own particular journeys toward freedom. Our experiences have great value. Even though it is difficult to see others in pain, we recognize the innate value of pain in our own lives, and therefore, we value it in the lives of others.

We each have within us the power to accomplish anything we want. The wisdom, strength, and spirit to create are uncovered as we look within to ask, "What do I want?" From there, we move forward to create those desires. People are not broken, incapable, or otherwise unable to live their own lives. There may be lots of trauma, drama, limiting beliefs, and hardened or darkened aspects of self, but freedom, light, love, and joy are possible. Abundance and prosperity are possible. The only way to show this to another human is to first become joyfully alive and joyfully abundant. When we believe in ourselves and discover our own ability to join desires with spirit, we understand that each person also has this potential.

Moving forward in our own excitement in an awakening dawn, we begin to recognize the possibility that more power is available than we ever dared imagine. For a while, we are like little children gazing at a winter wonderland scene, barely able to contain the awe we feel when we first witness that such magic exists. Not only does this mysterious wonderland exist, but it is ours to play in! Everything in life serves us. All energy aligns to bring our beliefs into physical form. It is always happening, even right now when we do not know how it is happening. Our individual journey is to discover how this world works. We can attend seminars or read books such as this one, but nothing can replace the necessity of taking action and applying concepts. We must learn for ourselves, within our own physical bodies, how to blend imagination, beliefs, and the spiritual aspect of who we are.

The mystery reveals itself as we move forward with open curiosity. If we want joy and if we seek joy, we will find that joy will serve us. There is nothing we need to push around. We do not need to eliminate sorrow; we only have to make room for

joy to expand. We can learn how to align with joy.

In this divine journey of self, we let ourselves have what is important to us. To do this, we first engage in learning the importance of feeling good. We learn how to draw power into our bodies, and we do not draw it from other people, but from our own spirit. We open up illustrious ideas or desired outcomes and pair these ideas with love. As we begin to understand that it is possible to create desired outcomes, our increase in personal power and love expand once again and exude outward, touching partners, family, friends, society, and countries all the way out to the planet and the universe.

Supporting ourselves in our enjoyment is a choice requiring practice and much patience. It is unfamiliar. We are used to living within old comfort circles, experiencing set quantities of excitement, joy, love, power, abundance, or inner peace. Our lives within the circles are maintained through old beliefs and mind strategies involving force, pushing at outcomes, and battling against things we do not want. Good fighting evil, evil fighting good, and old ideas fighting new ideas are the formerly learned ways of achieving goals that limit us. These ways of manifesting desires become outdated on our journeys of creation. Our journeys are now toward new lives of unlimited selves.

Being a warrior, holding power over others, using control or force is an available choice. However, we might recognize that this system does not feel good to those oppressed. It is not a win-win situation and love does not expand. Generally, though, seeing no other alternatives to create change, we either engage in this ineffective system or become disillusioned with life. Not knowing another method of motivation or success, we work harder, fight against the opposing forces, and push to achieve our goals. Certainly, we all want to become more than we are, to live the good life, and to feel good. If no other system of motivation is available, then we believe that force is the only alternative. Indeed, great outcomes can be achieved through force, but the price is high, leaving such feelings as despair or emptiness.

"Might makes right." This familiar term is an old system that is not morally wrong or bad, but it is a limiting choice. It is a system in which one aspect of self becomes empowered at the cost of another. On a larger scale, one person exerts power or control over another person. Or, one country becomes empowered over another, at a cost too painfully horrendous for most to acknowledge. People who use this system believe that power must be taken from another. Most people are accustomed to living their lives this way. In my heart and in every cell of my being, I know that authoritarianism, control, and manipula-

tion are never paths to greater joy, not even to those who are in control. Forcing ideas onto others or ourselves creates no expansion of joy. We do not expand power when we control, manipulate, or push ideas into achievement; we just move power around from one place to another.

Everyone adopts this system in one way or another. We attempt to control self, manipulate reality, and change others for the sake of our goals. We believe that what we want is external to us and must be obtained somehow. It is natural that we use force to fight against what we do not want because it is the system we have been raised in. There is another choice. Not everyone will decide to understand this alternative, but a great many people are moving themselves into becoming unlimited creators of a new Earth.

By recognizing the discomfort in our bodies, we dare to venture down the path of self-discovery to see what is inside. Deep within, we all find the same answers: ideas that seek to be exciting again, desires that enliven, new possibilities, and new potentials. Empowerment, love, and joy are unlimited resources and infinite in their abilities to expand, if we so choose. These energies come through us and through the love and acceptance of self. The mystery of life is that we create inside of ourselves first, through beliefs and imagination, and a connection of spirit and body, and then our creation

manifests in the physical world.

We have supported ourselves in disruption for a long time. It does not give us what we want. Motivation through worry, struggle, battle, and anxiety empowers feelings that we do not want to feel. Pushing ourselves through life does not bring more joy into our lives or the lives of those in the vicinity. It does not bring about more empowerment or the ability to share the expressions of our empowerment.

There is another system available to achieve dreams and to obtain success. We can choose to engage in bold concepts that contradict previous life lessons. We dare to believe that we are capable of imagining a desire, linking it with love, and allowing that desire to manifest. We intentionally play with the concept that we create *everything* inside before it appears outside. Exciting aspects of ourselves awaken, as the disruptive aspects of ourselves move out. This new choice also creates outcomes, but with the added benefits of expanded love, excitement, and empowerment. Love and power are not taken from one place and moved to another, but they are found within, expanded, and shared with our creative expression. Love is bigger than it was as we bring a new creative expression from within ourselves out into the world. Our bodies are capable of becoming living conduits of excited power and

creation. Standing in this wonderful physical lightness, we feel empowered and excited to be alive.

Understanding how creation works, we are able to share freely with others. In the past, we would fill our cups with energy each morning, head out into the world with a certain amount to give, and hope others would return the favor by giving energy back to us in the form of money, security, validation, or acceptance. In the evening, we would return home depleted, exhausted, and no longer enjoying our day-to-day existence. Now we understand that others are not the source of our love, joy, power, abundance, or prosperity. We understand we can become physically full, limitless cups of spiritual energy from the inside out. The more we share this energy into excited self-expressions, the more we are empowered. Nothing is given away, there is no depletion of energy, and there is no rescuing, no victim mentality, no martyring. There are no expectations that others should return energy, and there is no need to obtain energy from them.

There is power beyond the pushing and beyond the systems of struggle or force taught to us. Resistance and war are not the answers. The new choice is difficult to understand until we allow ourselves to exchange control for something far grander. Creation. The excitement caused by creation is the most amazing journey. This is how we design and implement a new world of peace, empowerment, love, and excitement, one human at a time.

It is not important to fight against disturbing situations, to engage in realities that do not excite us, or to end the world's problems. Instead, the magnificent journeys that will bring our illuminations into the world await us. We are made of love and light, ever and always. Our journeys are to share our love with ourselves first and then naturally with the world. Imagine no longer keeping our own brilliance invisible or subdued.

You may say you are no creative genius, but the truth is that we all are. Being creative means something different for everyone; it is an expression of individuality. Some will lean toward science or scholarship, others toward designing creative relationships, some toward inspiration, and others toward expression of artistic beauty. Creative individuals have the ability to both imagine and engage in fantasy while also being grounded and rooted. The human body is capable of becoming the conduit of joyful creation. Nothing can match the incredible feeling of joy in knowing we are powerful and capable of creating what we desire. We can create in a way that harms no one and disrupts no one, not even ourselves.

We have lived and believed in the duality of good versus evil

for so long. We need to risk looking beneath these ideas to uncover exciting ideas and new avenues of expression. We can release layers of self-protection, the layers of aged, heavy coats that were once warm and protective, but now are smothering in the new season of our lives. Beneath the fears and protections lie glimpses of how beautiful we are. How could we ever have believed otherwise? We came to Earth to be ourselves, and not to be the visions other people had for us. We are magnificent. It takes our breath away to discover the secret of self. Beneath the armor, the protection, the personality, and the mind are the most beautiful ideas ever witnessed, plus truths so indescribable that touching them brings tears of awe, inspiration, and amazement. Is this what we have covered up for so long?

It comes at first only in the briefest flicker. A veil lifts unexpectedly, and then drops as suddenly. In a brief moment, we witness the creative power available to us. Not only are our ideas magnificent and glorious, but we also have the power available to us to make those ideas come to life. These moments provide the motivation to journey further into truth. Our truths will never be found in another person, and they will never be found in any of the great books. This journey is not a logical journey and it is not one for the mind to understand beforehand. It is journey of valuing self to such a degree that love and power are brought into relationship with inner dreams. As we allow ourselves to receive the manifestation of those dreams, spirit is brought into physical form. What only existed first in the imagination, existed then in love, and now exists in physical form.

We all want to live great lives that feel good. Indeed life should be more than just a struggle. The enjoyment we seek comes only from knowing we hold the power to create what we want, including the joyful creation of money, success, or physical thinness—if that is what we want. One at a time, people are opening themselves to this new way of creation, leaving old battles behind, moving out the disruptive aspects of self, and filling up with exciting aspects of self. One person at a time, we decide that fighting the old world or thinking that external conditions must change first no longer serves our needs or the needs of humanity.

Living a joyful life requires loving self. Self-love is not so much an emotion as it is a diminishing absence of doubt and disapproval. It is a sense of balance and belonging. We cannot joyfully live in the physical world until we have first mastered joyfully living in our physical body. Self-love means that personal well-being matters unconditionally and in practical terms. Respect, responsibility for self, and feeling good are

important values. Primary objectives are fun, laughter, and taking the actions that increase overall enjoyment of life.

Self-love requires valuing personal ideas and expressing those ideas in ways that feel good. Who we are is important. What we want always matters. Self-love opens the door to loving others, and truly, we do not cease to love others when we place ourselves first. Children are not abandoned and partners are not left when we put self first. By making self a priority, we realize the importance of our relationships and now have greater energy and passion for making those aspects of life flourish.

We bring aspects of ourselves into physical expression through our creations. If we create from the essence of self, from love and spirit, then our creations gather themselves together with love and spirit. We dare to bring love, passion, excitement, and worthiness into our relationships with our dreams, even though they are initially ethereal, or non-physical. At first, our excitement is but a tiny speck of desire penetrating potential. Yet we continue to feed trust, devotion, repeated excitement, and imagination through the relationship portal of potential. These actions allow us to nourish our creations as they gather themselves together and expand. At some point in the process, our creations still exist within the ethereal womb of potential, but we can sense them becoming real.

They have gathered themselves together at our call and have created themselves from aspects of ourselves. The substance binding them together is the energy we offer, whether the energy is love or fear, receiving or force. Dreams are made of us, from and through us, but eventually they become separate entities. They continue to exist only in potential until we find ourselves worthy of receiving them into our lives. They must come through our bodies to move from the ethereal into this reality. A book is written through the body; a garden is imagined, planted, and tended through the body; a new body weight is created in the tissues of the body. If we love ourselves, if we love what we have created, if we trust ourselves to be worthy of creating in the world, we will bring these new lives into the physical world. We will nourish our creations until their completion. The book will find publication, a painting will be offered for viewing, or a newly created body will be held and maintained.

Beyond the Edge of Comfort

When the time arrives, when you acknowledge feeling bored, limited, trapped, bad, or hungry for something more, you are ripe to move forward into higher potentials. A readiness exists to wake up to the possibilities of creating new possible realities. Feelings of unease and discomfort serve important purposes. They tell you that you have traveled extensively into one expression of your being and have discovered all you care to discover. The adventure is no longer one you wish to continue. You explored a particular reality and witnessed for yourself the extent of available outcomes.

No matter how badly you are feeling because the end of one reality has been reached, there is no need for hatred of self, or hatred of current beliefs, habits, behaviors, or actions. Even if your life is filled with poverty, addictions, depression, or unhappy relationships, these are the outcomes of one potential. Your body is sending necessary signals of discontent, and you have the option of creating a new experience for yourself.

Your old life was neither disgusting nor shameful. It was perfect in its fully actualized state. Your experiences brought with them many important understandings and insight. You are as worthy of love, acceptance, and respect at this point in time as you are in any other point in time. When you began the journey that led you to this point, you did not know ahead of time where the adventure would lead. Now, in hindsight, the outcomes of certain beliefs, actions, and strategies are visible. This end point is not a place of failure, but a grand opportunity to collect the payment of your previous journey in the form of wisdom. This wisdom can then be applied to the creation of a new life experience.

You create change by acknowledging feelings of dissatisfaction and by accepting current realities. It is important to accept that somehow, unconsciously, you had the power to create whatever life you are living. Sure, there are aspects that are no longer acceptable, aspects that no longer serve you, and aspects you find disappointing, but there is absolutely no reason to hate others or yourself for having participated in life.

You assume responsibility and accept that you created the existing reality, not to torture or berate yourself, but because it is the only way to recognize your inner creative abilities and power. When you acknowledge the creator aspects of self, you release the beliefs that you are a victim of life, or a victim of other people's decisions. Did you consciously create the life you live? Probably not, but that does not mean you did not create it. It was created through deeply ingrained limiting beliefs, well-worn strategies, and habitual actions. Just imagine, if you can create entire realities based on unconscious beliefs and automatic strategies, what could you create if you experimented with the process of conscious creation? This awareness is the stepping-stone into new realities.

The causes of existing unhappy realities do not matter as much as the readiness and desire to create new realities. Nothing can be done to change what exists in this moment. Not even a supreme being could wipe out an event or feeling as if it had never happened. There is no need to wipe the slate clean. What is done is done. If you are willing to look, you will obtain important understandings. You held certain beliefs, created realities based on those beliefs, and then had opportunities to see the consequences unfold. There is no judgment, no right or wrong. You lived life with particular ways of believing and acting, and you had the physical experiences of seeing how they would turn out. If you are ready for change, it means you have seen the unfolding, witnessed the conclusions, and obtained wisdom. Now you are ready to move on. At any time, you can begin a new adventure that will lead to new consequences, new wisdom, and new understandings.

The time arrives in all lives to explore new potentials. You may ignore the signs, but they are there. While familiarity may seem sweet and comfortable, it can take the shine out of life. You can sense the readiness toward personal evolution when your body constantly tells you that you are not happy, you do not feel good, you are bored, and you do not have enough love or spirit flowing through you. The life you currently lead, with its available levels of joy and abundance, was created from limited sets of beliefs and actions. Everyone naturally and continuously outgrows old ways of being. Other potential realities can be created if you are ready to cultivate new beliefs and connect with joy. To do so requires you to be willing to take an adventure into the unknown.

What is in the unknown? Well, it is everything and nothing at first. You walk to the edge of your inner comfort circle and look out only to see a void. It is the presence of all potentials, but not yet any specific potential. Yet, within the void and past the edges of the comfort circle, there lies the possibility of all things. It is the place where nothing exists in any organized fashion, and yet the invisible ingredients of all things are floating around. You look into this void and wonder what your life could be if you were not so unhappy, shy, lethargic, depressed, poor, etc. You see nothing, and yet, within the void are the necessary components for creating any dream.

To create new potential realities, you must walk to the edge of the comfort circle, past the beliefs you currently hold, and dare to imagine what life would be like if you were joyful, healthy, outgoing, or abundant. Imagination is required to dream new dreams into creation. No one tells you what to create and your dream life is not already sitting out there. It is up to you to create anything you want to create. You feel excitement when you choose self-important dreams and ideas

that spark the flames of inner passion.

Our journeys always begin from within current comfort circles. They must, for nothing else yet exists. People try to fight current realities and try to make them go away. They believe that if they get rid of fat bodies, happiness will show up, or that if they struggle and push themselves into goals, then love, esteem, and worth will show up. It does not work that way. Hypothetically, even if we could somehow "get rid" of what exists, it would not matter because nothing new would have been created yet. By the very laws of life, we are responsible for the work of imagining what is wanted, aligning our desires with love, taking action, and allowing new potentials to form, before we can step into them.

For a moment, pretend to picture the comfort circle of your life. You are inside that circle. On the edge of the circle are many beliefs, some are optimistic, self-supporting, and exciting while others are self-limiting. All of these beliefs combine to create the life you are currently living within your circle. Beliefs lining the circle keep you safe and hidden inside. Nothing much changes and your general experiences keep repeating themselves. Whatever the beliefs are, they have created your current levels of abundance, joy, love, safety, etc. One day you outgrow your life inside the circle. You want to play a bigger role in life, be more empowered, more abundant, and more joyful. You want to have better relationships. You want a house instead of an apartment. You want to be self-employed instead of working for someone. Whatever it is, you realize that you want more than you had before.

Walking over to the edge of your comfort circles, you do not find a new Land of Oz already established. Your destiny is not sitting out there. A knight in shining armor is not waiting to come to your emotional rescue. You simply cannot simply cross out of your comfort circle into a larger life. You must spend time imagining a new larger life.

This is the tricky part: From inside your current life, filled with all its disruptions, emotions, beliefs, and manifestations, you must imagine something new, something you have never had before. They are imaginary potentials of living a healthier life with greater joy, passion, love, success, freedom, and abundance. But not only must you dream a general dream of having a "better" life, you are responsible to name what that more joyful life would look like to you. Your most joyful life would probably not be anything like my most joyful life.

As you stand on the edge of your circle, your imagined dreams are purely ethereal fantasies; they do not exist. You dream yourself to be wildly successful, abundant, and involved in an amazing relationship. You dream what all of those concepts

would look like to you. You dream this life from a place where you do not believe it is possible to have what you want. Every day you must make the effort to not focus so intently on the problems of your current existence. You must seek opportunities to prove to yourself that your current beliefs may not be the only truths available to you. Each day you must build new experiences to support the new beliefs, saying, "I can have what I want."

Throughout the process of change, you ask yourself to play imaginary games while deeply believing it to be impossible to achieve winning outcomes. If you are willing to engage in this act of deliberate creation, and stick with it until your desire is manifest, there will be many rewards along the way. You discover self-love in this journey as you learn the ability to lead yourself compassionately through doubt and hardships. You gain essential elements of worthiness, respect, and power. You discover the ability to give yourself intentional joy and excitement when needed most. Creating new dreams intertwined with new beliefs builds strong muscles of persistence. You must sit inside your old world and repeatedly visit your imagined new reality.

A lifetime of living by defined sets of beliefs will not change by repeating affirmations. Vigilance is the price you pay for freedom. You must consistently, throughout the day, moni-

tor yourself by asking, "How am I feeling about myself right now? Am I sitting in joy and expecting positive outcomes, or playing with stress and disruption? Am I taking the daily actions that feel good and support my dream?" If you are not feeling good, no harm done. Simply remind yourself to correct the situation by finding your dream and fanning the flames of desire once more.

Imagination is not a visual picture of what you want. It is a full body, full spirit experience. You take the time to create a living relationship with what you want, and each day you sit and internally create a completely new world right now. After that, the next crucial step must take place, and that is activating the imagined desire with spirit. In other words, you must breathe life into your desire. You must love your desire before it even exists. Only you carry the love necessary to weave the magic of spirit with inner desires. Your body will feel good as passionate ideas unfold and as your heart softens to caress your dreams. The good feelings do not arrive later in a priority package after you obtain what you want. The good feelings are necessary now. Love exists within you, and love allows all things.

Sometimes our imaginations are limited. We know exactly what we *do not* want. We can express and feel in vivid recollection every detail of what *does not* feel good, but the sense of

what we want, joy, abundance, health, love, etc., are drab and unfocused by comparison. Our imaginations lack the empowerment to focus on exact preferred outcomes. Rest assured, we do not have to know every detail before we begin, but a starting point is needed.

If, for example, a current relationship does not feel good, you can stop trying to figure out how to fix the other person. Going over the same argument for the one hundredth time is not going to produce a new outcome. Hoping the other person will change is not going to happen. And why should your partner be the one to change? You are the one who wants change, and therefore it is up to you to accept the responsibilities that come with change. It is up to you to go through the effort required.

If you have never seen a model of a great relationship, perhaps your imagination cannot come up with all the details. Do not allow this to become a deterrent. Start from this moment, right now, even with the smallest bit of information about what an exciting relationship would look like to you. How would you act? What would you be doing, saying, feeling, and experiencing? You can soften your heart to self for having this idea. Continue to play in the land of fantasy, remembering to bring the feelings of excitement up into the physical body. Creation involves the unified convergence of spirit and physical.

Something wondrous begins to happen. The old comfort circle of your life still exists, and you still exist within the circle. So outwardly, nothing in your life looks different yet. But, a new reality circle begins to form, slightly overlapping the old. This is a larger, more expanded circle encompassed by new beliefs, new ideas, and new potentials. At first, your new circle is faint and fuzzy. Each time you dare to love your dream, your new potential reality grows stronger and clearer. Each time you dare to feel yourself in a loving, harmonious relationship with your dream, your new potential reality grows stronger. You stand in your current physical reality, breathe deeply, and reach into the void joining imagination and love. You have dared yourself to see if you have such power. Are you truly capable of reaching into the void of all things, and can you assemble components of a new reality by yourself?

An Ending and a Beginning

You accomplished an amazing feat! From within your old reality, through persistence, patience, imagination, internal leadership, and excitement, you created a new possibility. You generated enough excitement and power to create what you wanted. A beginning has arrived, as has an ending. This is the anticipated triumph.

You still must decide to walk out of your old world, to release old beliefs, and to step into your new life. As magical as this changeover is, it can feel unexpectedly emotional. Up until this moment, you still have your comfortable, safe, well-known ways of life. Even though you have cultivated a new more exciting potential, you have not yet stepped into it fully.

In our previous example, the potential now exists for a more exciting relationship, but it does not yet exist in physical form. Perhaps your current partner does decide to change his or her ways and come with you on your journey, but perhaps they will not join you. They were content with the way things were. That is one problem with change. You can only create change in your own world; you cannot force someone else to change with you. In addition, the new cannot unfold before you release the old.

Do we dare gift ourselves with the possible physical manifestation of a new reality? How will it turn out? Will we survive if we let go of the old? This transition is emotional, as we have immense grief as we say goodbye to the strategies and behaviors of our old lives. Much to our amazement, this crossing-over place can be more difficult than we could possibly have foreseen. Immense love and patience are required to move from one reality into another.

We could be right on the edge of new lives, and unless we collapse and give up, something amazing is about to happen, but we will not know until we take one last courageous step. Aspects of self from which we created the new lives are jumping up and down with excitement and power. Listening to these voices, we realize that these new opportunities could be sweetly delicious and ecstatically enlivening, but sitting at the precipice of change are also the voices of the old, bringing with them adversity and conflicting thoughts. They speak loudly, demanding attention, drowning out the light of our dreams. These aspects are on determined missions designed to lure us back into the known. The new realities are, after all, their worst fears. These parts of ourselves were quite content with the old ways. They liked the relative safety of living in the known and familiar. They have no desire to take a journey into uncharted territories. Being caught in the voices of unbounded fears robs us of the energy we need in order to complete the transitions. Temptation lures us to retreat.

On these edges of transition, the voices of old lives ensnare us like Greek Sirens. The ache of their genuine call descends thick and dark, clinging tentacles clutching at us to remain in the familiar. Tumultuous and unrestrained, loud voices weeping and wailing, they demand that we remain in the safety of what we have always known. They are angered and enraged,

hypnotizing, deceiving us with anguish, frustration, and fear. Spellbound, our fear seems so absolute. Caught off guard by these unexpected and unanticipated occurrences, we fall into the depths of dark fear. Unable to find balance and to leave the voices of fear behind, we are lost to our fears.

In mythology, the Sirens lived on three small, rocky islands. They sang irresistibly seductive songs to enchant sailors and their ships to the island's jagged rocks. Once shipwrecked on the rocks, the men would drown as they dove overboard to join the Sirens. In mythology, both Odysseus and the Argonauts encountered Sirens in their adventures. Their songs, so beguiling, would have caused Odysseus to steer his ship into their rocks. To avoid this temptation and deception, Odysseus plugged the ears of all his men with beeswax. To resist temptation by the seduction of the Sirens' songs, he had himself tied to the mast of his ship. Through this leadership plan, he avoided a shipwreck on the rocks.

In another myth, when the Argonauts were about to pass the islands of the Sirens, they did so with the aid of Orpheus, who was a great poet and musician, master of the lyre. His music and singing could charm wild beasts, coax the rocks and trees into dance, and even arrest the courses of rivers. At the appropriate time, Orpheus provided distraction by playing such beautiful music on his lyre that the Sirens' songs were drowned out. The ship safely passed without smashing into the rocks of destruction. In both myths, the danger was recognized and anticipated. Utilizing essential leadership to ensure the success of the mission, plans occurred ahead of time to deal with a predictable obstacle.

The bewitching voices of our fears would have us veer off course and collide into the jagged rocks of the unknown. We would not die, but we would never experience the dreams we so lovingly created. Will we surrender to those voices that formerly kept us living small and fearful, or will we draw on the power of the new to guide us through? The old voices contain only fear, fictions, and lies. There is no greatness within them, no passion, and no radiance or beauty. How do we get by these voices? Odysseus and the Argonauts recognized that there was no way to stop the songs of the Sirens. The way forward involves not avoidance of painful fears, but a prepared journey into and through them. The fears are not going to go away, but there are ways to resist the temptation to retreat. Like Odysseus and the Argonauts, we must find ways to stay determined and on course, to tie ourselves down, to remain grounded, and to fill our ears with beautiful music. The same grace, acceptance, love, and self-leadership that brought us to this point are now needed more than ever to help us resist retreat.

The lure of the past is engulfing, but there are ways to stay focused on what is important. The first thing you need to do is to recognize what has happened. Although this downward spiral into fear was unforeseen, it is typical. The enormous outpouring of fear occurred because you succeeded. You created new destinies through dreams, imagination, and love. These new destinies hold the promises of power, excitement, and greater lives. The only thing remaining for you to do is to take a step of faith. You will end up in desired places, but it cannot happen unless you take the step.

For those of us not much into thrill-seeking or steps of faith, this transition can be paralyzing. If possible, seek guidance from objective friends who can offer much needed support and perspective. You might be disappointed or surprised at the anger you feel when your friends do not tell you everything you want to hear. Generally, you want to have your old beliefs validated; however, objective people are not likely to do it. Instead, they will remind you to not panic, and they will emphasize the importance of finding your confidence, footing, and balance. They will tell you to be cautious of retreating from such a good thing. Your dreams were important when you imagined them, trusted them, and believed them into being. Your dreams are still important. Objective parties also remind you that the option of listening to your doubts and fears is always available. There is no need to move forward except for your own need to know what lies ahead.

Before giving in completely to your fears, notice how dark they are. There is no brilliance, no radiance, no love, and no power to be found in the voice of fear. You need great self-leadership, in whatever ways possible, to find openings back into your dreams, for within your dreams lie the excitement and power you want and need so much. Your dreams will provide the confidence to face doubts and to move forward. You can use whatever tools available to pull out of the grasp of your fears and regain solid footing. Recall your dreams; they, like Orpheus, will sing songs more beautiful than those your fears sing, distracting you from the voices of impending doom. Your dreams will lift up your heart, coaxing you once more into movement.

Only your dreams hold the excitement and energy you need to take the final steps into a new reality. Your dreams are what save you from the tantrums being thrown by aspects of yourself that want to keep you safe in your fixed identity. The excitement of your dreams is the only energy strong enough to get you through the process of change. It ties you to the mast, grounds and balances, and overrides the voices of fear. Excitement is the inner energy available to you to keep your

attention fixed and focused on success. Trust that your future reality will be a good reality because you dreamed it to be a good reality.

Spirit and Human United

You are a spirit with a physical body, not a body with a spirit. Yet, as long as you are on Earth, you do have a body. The kind of association you have with your body is up to you. You may ignore it, hate it, or think it is the source of all your suffering. You may view it as an unconnected foreign object that you are forced to walk around in. You may believe that critical thoughts, aches and pains, depression, stress, and anxiety are things that are being done to you. However, if you adopt the position that you are a spirit that has an awesome opportunity to live in a physical body and enjoy physical experiences, then you can consciously interrelate with your body and feel good in this reality.

Have you ever really stopped and thought about it? What do you need in order to feel good? The answer lies in spirit. Possessions, money, and accomplishments do not make you happy. What makes you happy is how much spirit you put into the process of creating possessions, money, or accom-

plishments. When you bring spirit into your life and into your physical body, you do things with a sense of flow and with feelings of joy. It does not matter if you are washing dishes, vacuuming, or closing multi-million dollar deals. The only thing that matters is how much spirit you bring to the process. The outcomes of processes are not so much the point. The time between now and then is the point. If you bring spirit into the process, then the time between now and then is joyful.

Focusing on your dreams, loving your dreams, allows you to feel good because it engages your spirit. You feel good when you actively line up with inner dreams, preferences, desires, and values. You stand within yourself, and you are not opposed to any other opinions or dreams, but firmly committed to your own. Your dreams excite you, and you do things for your own sake, feeling good in the process rather than for the success or money that the outcomes bring. You allow yourself to utilize excitement to generate the required energy to follow through and achieve success.

Self-loving people actively work on feeling good. It is not something someone else is supposed to give to you. No one can hold you from the connection with your own spirit. Feeling good is something you allow. It rises up from the inside because you decide that is what you want. It does not come

from the outside in. Feeling good is a personal responsibility and is something you learn to value and allow. It takes deliberate effort and practice. If you are used to being tossed about by your emotions like a ship on a stormy sea, it is time to decide to take charge and learn how to feel good.

Having exciting ideas feels wonderful. No matter what problems are going on or what fears have most recently filled your body, you have choices. It is going to take some motivation and some work, but you have the choice to shift from thinking about things that feel bad to thinking about exciting ideas that feel good. In this moment, right now, you can take time to sort through some ideas until you find one that feels good and that brings a spark of life. The initial result is feeling good. The long-term result is much grander. Learning how to focus with excitement and intention on what you want creates desired outcomes.

Your body never lies. It clearly tell you what feels good and what does not feel good. When you acknowledge what the pain is all about, then remove attention from painful thoughts and beliefs, and stand solidly in exciting imagined outcomes, your body begins to feel good. You connect with self, open your heart, and energy flows through you. Your feel empowered. This energy is now available to fuel action and to create the expressions of dreams and desires.

Sometimes others share their energy with us. For instance, acquaintances can provide much needed love, encouragement, acceptance, or praise when we are feeling unsure about ourselves. They can provide companionship and comforting touch when we feel alone. Friends may give energy as they laugh and play with us, and companions may speak loving words, offer soft caresses, or hold us while we hurt. Partners give us energy when they listen to our sorrows. They quietly allow us to be where we are without fixing or rescuing us. Nurses, counselors, body workers, therapists, healers, and good friends are often sources of much-needed loving energy. Sometimes, when we are feeling down and low, we need supportive relationships to offer us energy to give us little boosts up out of our funks.

Accepting energy from others is part of how life works. This energy is beautiful when someone else shares it willingly. There is pleasure in sharing energy, and there is pleasure in receiving energy. A huge problem arises when we believe energy, such as love, praise, motivation, excitement, joy, or feeling good, is available only from outside ourselves or through other people. This concept is the source of much of our suffering. If others are the sources of what we need, we end up developing unique ways of trying to capture that energy. People pleasing, rescuing, righteousness, or being sick can all be attempts to control

and manipulate others into giving us what we need. When they do not willingly share, we may pout, become angry, or find other strategies to outsmart them, or we might find others who will be more easily conned into giving us the energy we need. We are not bad people because we unconsciously attempt to gain energy. We all need a constant source of energy running through our bodies.

Getting energy from outside sources is not the ultimate answer. That system is laden with limitations and problems. First, it takes many strategies to get energy from another person. It means winning the available energy for ourselves at the expense of others. Second, the other person may or may not want to give us their energy. When they do not give us the energy we want, we typically find some form of retaliation. Finally, energy from a source outside ourselves is finite and never enough.

For example, people stuck in "helpless victim" roles will seek out others who will provide energy through rescuing attempts. The "helpless victims" have no real incentive to get well because at some level they are getting the much-needed attention and energy they require. There is always another friend, therapist, counselor, or alternative healer available to feed the need. A person getting high will continue to seek the next high. A person addicted to sex searches for the next

sexual affair to satisfy them. The person who binges cannot get enough. The person searching for money to fill them up never feels wealthy or full. Money, food, sex, gambling, shopping, alcohol, and drugs may all be wonderful experiences in the right context, but none satisfies if the *reason* for getting them is to fill an internal need.

Everyone needs energy in order to survive. The strategies people develop in order to capture some much-needed energy are not in any way bad; they are just limited. In addition, our strategies do not feel good on a larger scale. The immediate "fix" may feel good, but the consequences are often undesirable. In contrast, the energy each person needs to feel good is always available within and in unlimited quantities. We do not need to play games with ourselves or other people to get it. There is no need to please another person so they will accept us and offer much needed energy. We do not need to be pretty, thin, rich, or acceptable so that the world will hopefully offer the love we seek.

The energy, the excitement, and the power you want will arise from the passions of inner dreams and desires. Softening your body to new thought forms of feeling good, you discover that excitement and power were always available within. Passion is the excitement you feel in your belly. Passion shows itself in the outcomes you imagine or activities you engage in that feel

good overall, not just in the short-term. Love is the energy of your heart sharing itself with your gut-level passions. When you open up and find yourself worthy of allowing yourself to be your own source of feeling good, you no longer need to rely on other people to give you what you want. This does not leave you alienated and alone, but free to be yourself and easily accept others for whom they are.

Imagine what your life would be if you knew that within yourself is the power to feel good and generate what you most want. What if you absolutely knew that all expressions of creation are possible? Imagine life if you knew that you are not trapped here on Earth, not just spending time waiting to go to a "better" place, not forced to be living in a body, and certainly not powerless. Imagine if you knew that you would have to go through a learning curve, but you could discover how to create an exciting life, and through the process, feel vibrant, alive, and peaceful. The outcomes of such scenarios would be that you would consciously create your version of paradise on Earth.

This new reality is possible, but it will not happen by itself. It happens with choice and a desire to feel good. It happens when we consciously decide to stop filling ourselves with disruption, stress, anxiety, and arguing, and when we stop attempting to reach goals through force and pushing. Within us all are ideas

of rage, cynicism, bitterness, animosity, hatred, and lack of abundance. These are not bad thoughts, and we are not bad for having them, but staying trapped in these strategies and fixated on them with inflexible minds locks us in bodies that do not feel good.

Uncomfortable beliefs, emotions, and strategies are indicators that we have lost touch with our own spirits, and they speak to us through our bodies, saying, "This is what we don't want." This is important information. What is equally important is the ability to step out of stress and into a more resourceful state and utilize this information to imagine an outcome that feels good right now. We get to choose how we will feel. We get to choose whether we will be pessimistic about our life, or whether we expect positive outcomes.

Love is the desire to feel good most of the time. When we love ourselves, we take the time to stop playing and poking at problems, and instead open ourselves to creative solutions. Love is about being alive and being excited about being alive. It is being so in love with ourselves that the most important thing is feeling good until one day our excitement overflows into this reality. Life can be a nightmare, or it can be a paradise. The choice has always been ours, even if we did not know it.

We carry the power to ignite this reality and to ignite power in those who wish for empowerment. This is what we came here to do; not to commiserate or dissociate from those who are not empowered; not to feel pity for the sick, the poor, or the sad; not to rescue others or even join them. We came here to lift ourselves up out of our own oppressive energies, to carry greater excitement and power, and to become intimate with our ability to create with spirit in a physical world. First, we become excited in our own lives, forging light in our bodies, light in our relationships, and light in our lives. We flow with the abundance and the joy of our own lives. We become the embodiments of joyful beings.

For a moment, imagine something exciting for yourself. If you could not fail, if you were not scared, if you were not holding yourself back, what ideas would you find exciting? Now settle on one and fill up with this idea. When you become a body so filled with an exciting idea and so filled with excitement and love, you experience the fact that the boundaries between the physical plane and the spiritual plane combine. Simply allow what you want without any pushing, worrying, or fretting. Your body is soft, relaxed, imagining, excited, and you say, "This is what I choose. I find myself worthy of receiving what I choose. I am supported in what

I choose." Throughout this little exercise, play and imagine to such an extent that you and your body begin to feel really good, both grounded and light.

That is it. Creating change could be as basic as practicing this one minute, full-body, full-spirit exercise multiple times each day. Intentionally switch attention to this warm, loving, and exciting imagined life every time worry, stress, or critical thoughts arise. Sounds simple, right? It may be simple, but whether or not it is easy is another story. This shortcut to feeling good goes counter to most of the beliefs we hold, so it may sound strange and unbelievable.

Grand miracles happen when we become excited about living and being in our bodies. This requires being open to the idea that life can be a rich adventure full of joy. It also requires releasing attachments to suffering, worrying, and feeling stress, while attaching to thoughts and actions that evoke inspiration. Imagine the influence of you, living in the joy of who you are, comfortable in your own skin, and oozing with appreciation and gratitude for life. Imagine living every breath in gratitude, filled with thanks and blessings for an amazing life. Imagine not losing compassion for those who do not know that they need not be victims, but instead realizing the best way to help them is to lift yourself up.

Love is the potential that exists for *one* person to live an exciting life; one person who is willing to trade suffering, stress, addiction, poverty, or depression for a joy-filled life and joy-filled creations; one person who is willing to choose to know the unthinkable; one person who decides not to fear their own ideas or their own body. Imagine spirit and human united, and the love of this union spreading unstoppable into the universe. Believe the enjoyment of life is possible. Believe a loving world filled with abundance, joy, prosperity, and health is possible. That world begins inside you and creates itself through you. You are that highest potential.

Once a long time ago, a little girl stood at the edge of a garden. Warm tears welled up in her eyes, her heart saddened because she did not know how to bring light and love to this world. The little girl grew up. She journeyed far and wide, and she took many divergent paths in her search. She did not know quite what she was looking for, or how to go about finding it. At times she strayed far and grew cold, depressed, and tired. These moments taught her to adjust her course and to travel in new directions. She climbed over hills and valleys, and then she descended down through the dark abyss. It is true that if one seeks, one finds. In time, she learned to trust her life, spirit, heart, and intuition. Slowly she found her way back home, into her own body, and into her own inner

dreams. When she arrived, she uncovered the answer she had always sought. She was surprised how the answer could be so complex and yet so simple . . . become the dream.

About the Author

Annette Colby, Ph.D., is an internationally known consultant, educator, and visionary author. Her contagious passion for life is shared in her writing and private practice where she inspires people to believe in themselves and find themselves worthy of receiving their dreams. She opens the doorway that leads to the brave new path of exploring the finest possibilities of life. For over two decades, she has been committed to showing people how to lovingly create inner dreams and desires, enjoy excited physical aliveness, and live with a connection to personal spirit truth and life purpose. She lives in Dallas, Texas, with her husband Ray and their two feline companions.